RENOVATE

Renovate
Building a Life with God

Renovate
978-1-5018-4336-5
978-1-5018-4337-2 *eBook*

Renovate: Leader Guide
978-1-5018-4338-9
978-1-5018-4339-6 *eBook*

Renovate: DVD
978-1-5018-4340-2

The Connected Life
Small Groups That Create Community

This handy and helpful guide describes how churches can set up, maintain, and nurture small groups to create a congregation that is welcoming and outward-looking. Written by founding pastor Jacob Armstrong with Rachel Armstrong, the guide is based on the pioneering small group ministry of Providence United Methodist Church in Mt. Juliet, Tennessee.

978-1-5018-4345-7
978-1-5018-43464 eBook

Also by Jacob Armstrong:

Interruptions
Loving Large
The God Story
Treasure: A Four-Week Study on Faith and Money
Upside Down

With Jorge Acevedo:
Sent: Delivering the Gift of Hope at Christmas

With James W. Moore:
Christmas Gifts That Won't Break: Expanded Edition with Devotions

With Adam Hamilton and Mike Slaughter:
The New Adapters

RENOVATE
BUILDING A LIFE WITH GOD

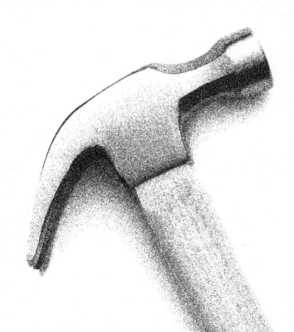

JACOB ARMSTRONG

Abingdon Press
Nashville

RENOVATE

BUILDING A LIFE WITH GOD

This book is printed on elemental chlorine-free paper.

Library of Congress Cataloging-in-Publication Data has been requested.
ISBN 978-1-5018-4336-5

17 18 19 20 21 22 23 24 25 26 — 10 9 8 7 6 5 4 3 2 1

MANUFACTURED IN THE UNITED STATES OF AMERICA

To Mary—

*Your birth and life have shown me more about God
than you will ever know*

CONTENTS

Introduction.......................................11

1. Never Too Late for a Renovation 19

2. Crying and Building............................37

3. What to Know Before You Build...................57

4. When Others Don't Like Your Plans 75

5. Inviting Others to Come Home 93

6. The Big Reveal...............................109

Acknowledgments 123

Introduction

INTRODUCTION

I met Nehemiah in 2007. I had heard his name before. I had read his story a handful of times. At some point, I understood his historical significance and his place in the biblical story. But I had never spent any time with him.

I've learned you can have a lot of information about people and still not really know them. That was me and Nehemiah up until the summer of 2007. I didn't meet him until I was at the end of my rope. I was twenty-seven. I was searching. That's when my renovation started.

The renovation introduced me to Nehemiah and began a journey I'm still on today. Meeting Nehemiah wasn't like meeting Jesus. I'm not talking about salvation here. Well, I guess a salvation of sorts, but not the one that we normally talk about and that we all need. I don't mean salvation from our sins and the new life in Christ. For me, meeting Nehemiah began an understanding of how, broken and disconnected as all of us are sometimes, I could be rebuilt in a way that my life might be lived for God. That meeting showed me that some of the things stirring around in me weren't just fragments of my own neurosis and insecurity. There was some of that for sure, but God had put a stirring in me to be reborn, rebuilt, and renovated. That stirring would introduce me to a hope and a wholeness I had not yet experienced.

My renovation began with a question, a breakdown, and a commitment.

The question came from God. I didn't get a *Field of Dreams* voice in a cornfield, but I believe it was the voice of God all the same. It was a question in my heart. A question I couldn't shake. A question that shook me.

"Will you go wherever I want you to go?"

I first heard it in Atlanta. I was in a season marked by persistent restlessness. I had gone to about as much school as you can go to. I had made a plan for my life that I was living into with precision and skill. I was doing all the things I was supposed to be doing. And it wasn't cutting it. I sensed there was more. I felt that God had something else for me. But I had no idea what it was. I was restless. I also had quite a bit of brokenness, unacknowledged and unaddressed. I was pretty sure I was having a quarter-life crisis.

Instead of buying a Corvette, I found myself in Atlanta leading a group of college students at a conference. That weekend, around every street corner and in every quiet moment, I felt God asking: "Will you go wherever I want you to go?" In some ways the question scared me, and in other ways the question annoyed me. It annoyed me because I had told God over and over again what I was going to do with my life. I had spelled it out to God and asked God to sign in agreement that my plan was a good one. So, why was God pestering me with a question that surely would lead to more uncertainty, indecision, and restlessness? That's what scared me. I wasn't sure I could handle much more.

I returned to our hotel room one night, and Rachel, my beautiful wife of five years at the time, calmly said, "Hey, can we talk?"

"Sure," I said.

She said, "I feel like God is asking us a question. I can't shake it."

"Oh, really?" I responded. I could feel it coming. As nonchalantly as I could I asked, "What's the question?"

But I could have said it along with her, word for word. I knew that the question God was asking me would be the question God was asking her. That evening, at that Holiday Inn Express, in the voice of my most beloved friend, I heard God ask me again:

"Will you go wherever I want you to go?"

It put me on my knees. I thought I had answered the question before. Meaning: I thought I had told God my life was not my own. I thought I had surrendered. I had sung, "Take my life, and let it be consecrated, Lord, to thee." But I see now that it wasn't until that night, in that hotel room, that I finally opened myself up to the renovation.

That was the question. Next came the breakdown. It is not easy to give up a self-focused, years-in-the-making plan for your life. It does not just float out of your fingers into the waiting hands of God. At least not for me. It hurt.

I wrestled with the question for a few weeks. (I take after my biblical namesake.) Then I decided to get away for a few quiet days to sort things out with God. I traveled to Holy Trinity Monastery, near my brother's house in the desert of southern Arizona. (I tend to make everything dramatic.) I decided that being silent in a place where I could hear only God's voice would be the best way to find out what God wanted to do with me.

The wheels of my brother's truck turned up a cloud of dust as he left me in the desert with the monks. My stomach turned with the thought of spending days by myself in silence. I had come to be quiet, and almost immediately my mind was filled with noise. With each passing minute that inner noise grew louder.

The silence was eating at me. It started to devour me. My old tricks weren't available. There was nowhere to go and nothing to do. I tried. I went to the monastery library and in one sitting read a book on the Benedictine Rule. It didn't work. No accomplishment or achievement could drown out that inner noise.

I went and sat down by a river, a tributary of the Rio Grande that ran behind the monastery. There, I had to listen to all my insecurities. I had to pay attention to some wounds that had been festering. I had to breathe. And it was there that I had my breakdown. I cried. I prayed. I wrote furiously, then set the pen down. I took a nap on the gravelly bank. I woke up and talked to God. Sounds like a pretty good breakdown, huh? It was.

It turned out that the question—"Will you go wherever I want you to go?"—wasn't really about a physical place or a new job or a life accomplishment on the horizon. It was about submitting my life to God in a way I had not experienced before. It was about a beautiful renovation that God wanted to do in me.

Yes, it led to a different physical place. It led to a new job. It led to accomplishments that we now celebrate. But to start with, it was about hearing God's question, like the question you may be hearing right now, so that God can work wonders. To heal you and rebuild you, to renovate your life.

I made a commitment that day. I made it there in silence, then brought it back to my noisy life in Nashville. I committed to let God do whatever God wanted to do, to allow God to rebuild my life. And in so doing to trust that what God would build in and through me would be beautiful and good.

That's when I met Nehemiah. I stumbled upon him in my reading, and he stopped me in my tracks. I realized that I was Nehemiah. Nehemiah was me. His story was my story.

Nehemiah heard God ask him a question. He had a major breakdown. Out of the breakdown he answered God's call and committed himself to a journey that is still the journey of all who follow God. Nehemiah's renovation wasn't just about him; no God-ordained renovation is. It's always about the renovation of God's people. Be assured that God is leading you on a course that will be about so much more and so many more people than just you. Trust me, that's a good thing.

As part of my own journey, God led me to start a new church in 2007, and this book is about what that church and I have learned from Nehemiah. We have studied and prayed through his story again and again, and each time we see ourselves in a new way. Which should be no surprise. Nehemiah's story is the story of God's people, who find themselves in desperate need of some help. They are restless. They are broken. And God uses the restlessness and brokenness of one to speak to them all. God uses Nehemiah to rebuild the people of God, and in so doing God rebuilds Nehemiah.

God has a question for you, some way of asking, "Will you submit your life to me?" I would guess that God has a breakdown for you; I know that God has healing for you; and out of that experience God will set you on a journey that is for your good and the good of others.

If I have learned anything from the story of God's people, it is that God has a renovation in store for you. You are a spiritual house, and God is ready to start the renovation.

1.

Never Too Late
for a Renovation

1. NEVER TOO LATE FOR A RENOVATION

You also, like living stones, are being built into a
spiritual house.

(1 Peter 2:5a)

I was in the sanctuary, sitting up front in one of the big high-back chairs, like thrones really, when Andrew walked in the back doors of the sanctuary. The service had already started, and we stood to sing one of the great hymns of the church. The organ was blaring, the pipes right behind me, I could feel the sound. I was a pastor on staff at a large traditional church. There were many people in the room that day, but I couldn't miss Andrew.

He entered wearing black tennis shoes, black shorts, a black Metallica shirt, and a black hat. (He was also wearing black socks, in case you were wondering.) This was far from the normal attire for Sunday services at First United Methodist Church. He was a young man who appeared to be in his early twenties, and he walked all the way down the middle aisle to the second row. He set his Starbucks coffee down on the seat next to him, obviously having missed the clearly marked signs as he entered that said "No food or drink in the sanctuary." As we stood and sang, he proceeded to take off his shoes, prop them up on the pew in front of him, and drink his coffee. It was like he had come to observe this strange thing that we knew of as a church service.

Fearing for his life, I began to pray for him. I pictured the ushers rappelling down from the balcony to hustle him out of the room. OK, not really, but I was worried that someone would say something rude about his sock feet or his hat or his coffee or... well, there were a lot of things. A few of my preconceived notions about that historic church were dispelled that day, because not one person said anything of the sort. In fact, he came back the next week and the next week and the next, and all he received was a warm welcome.

I really wanted to talk to him. He had piqued my curiosity for sure. But each Sunday he would slip out the way he came in, right down the middle aisle during the final hymn. Every week I tried to catch him, but every week he was gone. Finally, on his fifth or sixth week with us, instead of walking out during that final hymn he walked forward, toward the altar that was rarely used. There he bent his knees and knelt, just like he knew what an altar rail was for, and he sobbed. It was my moment to meet this mystery guest. I got to him first, and, as I put my hand on his shoulder, his body heaved under heavy cries. He really couldn't say much. I said a brief prayer and asked him if we could have lunch soon. He said yes.

The next day, over a sub sandwich, I learned Andrew's name. After a couple hours of conversation I asked him, "What do you think about Jesus?" To this day his response is stuck in my brain and heart.

"No one has ever told me about Jesus," he said.

We started talking about Jesus, and over the next days and weeks God continued the renovating work in Andrew's heart, work that surely began long before he decided to walk into the sanctuary with his Starbucks.

Some months later Andrew called me, and he was crying again. I met him at church, and we sat in the darkened sanctuary, on the back row this time, the moon giving a beautiful glow to the red stained-glass windows. Andrew was ready for a change. He wanted something different in his life. He wanted broken things to be rebuilt. He wanted Jesus. In the same place where he had mustered the courage to come in the "wrong" clothes, in the "wrong" way, knowing none of the prescribed customs and practices, Andrew came again that night with courage and vulnerability. In the same place where I had worried he would feel unwelcome or perhaps even be run off, he was welcomed and given space. In that same place, Jesus welcomed him and began one of the most dramatic renovation projects I have ever witnessed.

It had nothing to do with clothes or coffee. As long as I knew Andrew, he kept the same wardrobe and carried the same coffee cup. That wasn't the change I'm talking about. I witnessed that young man's heart being healed and encouraged and built back up. For me as a young minister, Andrew had a profound effect on my understanding of how Jesus can come in and work a miracle in a heart. That experience with Andrew was a precursor to the renovating work of God in my own life. I realized I, too, needed what Andrew was experiencing.

Did you know that God describes us as houses?

Often God employs images to help us understand the depth and mystery of the not-easy-to-explain spiritual stuff. Jesus did it all the time. He would use a story, a picture, an image to communicate how the supernatural connects with the natural. One frequently used image, often overlooked, is of a house. I am a house. You are a house. But it's more than that. We are God's houses.

Paul put it like this: "We co-workers in God's service; you are God's field, God's building." Later he asks, "Don't you know that you yourselves are God's temple and that God's spirit dwells in your midst?" (1 Corinthians 3:9, 16).

Peter wrote that "you also, like living stones, are being built into a spiritual house" (1 Peter 2:5).

Building, temple, house. For God.

If we embrace the image of spiritual house, then we can begin to consider what renovation work might be needed. Many of us would say our exterior looks good (well, at least OK) but our interior is a mess! In fact, our interior may be such a mess that we're left with the same old questions: Where do I start? How do I start? It is with these very questions that a God-size renovation can begin. After all, renovations are most needed in messy places—places that are in need of being cleaned out and built again.

Admitting our interior mess raises an awkward and embarrassing fact: We don't want anyone else to know the state of our souls! It's sort of like how we feel when someone drops by to visit our house unannounced. Personally I love having people come over, but I also appreciate a heads-up phone call beforehand. Why? Because I don't want you to see how I kick off my shoes when I sit on the couch and sometimes don't pick them up until the next morning. I'd rather you didn't know that each week we set stuff on the counters until they are full, and then we pile things on the dinner table, so that by Friday it looks like we poured out the contents of our mailbox and the girls' backpacks on every available surface.

All right, the truth? Most days it looks like a bomb was detonated in our bonus room, our golden retriever's hair covers everything, and our girls' bathroom...it's just bad. So visiting my house and having a glass of tea on the front porch is no big deal. But coming inside...oh, please, call first.

Most of us, not wanting others to see our messy interior, get a little uncomfortable thinking that God may want to do a full-on renovation in us and through us. I get it. We have a warm feeling when we hear the story of Andrew and his vulnerable walk to the altar, but it's a whole different story when we think about opening up and coming forward like that.

But what if we did open up? What if God's work isn't limited to young people who gather the courage to approach the altar? What if God has a renovation for each of us, but we have never allowed ourselves to dream about it?

The Fixer-Upper

There is currently a fascination with renovating homes, namely the so-called fixer-uppers. A fixer-upper, if you don't know, is a house that can be lived in but everyone knows it needs some work. Most of the time it needs a lot of work. Chip and Joanna Gaines are the stars of the highly-rated hit TV show, *Fixer Upper*. Chip and Joanna have renovated hundreds of homes and in fact live in a fixer-upper themselves. Joanna brings the vision for the renovation, and Chip makes it happen. They are charming and witty and have great teeth. In each episode, they help home buyers look past the dilapidated state of an old home and ultimately transform it into a dream home. In forty minutes or so, not counting commercials, a house goes from a mess to being the envy of all the neighbors.

The popularity of the show has coincided with another craze: DIY, or do-it-yourself. This isn't the first time that we've found ourselves fascinated with fixing things ourselves. Bob Vila and Tim "Tool Man" Taylor paved the way for Chip and Joanna. As a result, a whole new generation of unqualified people are injuring themselves and damaging their homes. Kidding, sort of. But however you describe it, there is a lot of energy and money being spent on trying to turn our houses into dream homes, all by ourselves.

In chapter 2 I'll introduce you to Nehemiah, who will help us follow a renovation project from its beginning to its grand unveiling. But first I want to share a few things to keep firmly in mind.

You are God's house, and God cares about
the inside of the house.

I'm not sure if God cares that your shirt is pressed or your hair is just right. But the inside? Oh, God cares so much about the inside. And most of our insides, if we are honest, are fixer-uppers. Some of us need a little work here and there. Some of us need a full renovation.

If you pay close attention to what Jesus told his disciples and the crowds that followed him, you will notice again and again that his concern was about the inside. In the longest continuous collection of Jesus' teachings that we have, the Sermon on the Mount, Jesus pushed us to examine our hearts. He mentioned old law after old law that focused on outward actions and did not honor God. Do not murder. Do not commit adultery. Jesus said that with each outward action, we should also be concerned about what's inside, such as the anger in our heart or the lust in our mind. Outward actions are important, of course, but actions flow from the inside. When we begin to see ourselves as a renovation project, we must realize that God will start on the inside.

In college, I spent a few summers as an intern with a program that did renovation and repair work on homes in lower-income neighborhoods around the campus. I loved it. I loved being part of a process in which something fragile became strong again, even beautiful again. Projects involved such jobs as rehabbing floors, putting on new roofs, and installing wheelchair ramps. I felt like I was making a difference.

On one project, we were putting new shingles on a roof for a woman in her late fifties who lived alone. Her name was Barbara.

It was a pretty simple job for us—so simple, in fact, that our regular foreman left me in charge with some teenagers from out of state who had come to join the work.

The first afternoon, one of the teenagers needed to use the restroom. I told her to ask the nice woman who owned the home if she could go inside. When the teenager returned a few minutes later, she was wide-eyed and a little shaken up. She described the inside of the house, and I went to take a look for myself. It was the first time I saw what is called "hoarding." The entire house was overflowing with stuff. Waist-high piles of trash and old furniture filled the house. There were narrow trails through the house so you could walk. The smell was almost unbearable.

We had done a comprehensive assessment of the outside of her house, even started our work, and all the while the inside was barely habitable. We hadn't noticed. I sat on the front porch with Barbara, and we talked about the inside of her house. She began to cry. She said she wanted help but had no idea where to start. I didn't either. New shingles we could handle, but this house needed much, much more. It wasn't a do-it-yourself project. It was beyond the scope of our mission program. Chip and Joanna would never take this job.

We knew that no matter what we did to make the outside of Barbara's house better and stronger, if we did nothing to address the inside we were wasting our time.

Your renovation is not a do-it-yourself project.

This book is about a rebuild, a restoration, a renovation. It ain't DIY. Peter, who wrote that we are spiritual houses, closed his letter with these words:

*The God of all grace, who called you to his
eternal glory in Christ, after you have suffered
a little while, will himself restore you and make
you strong, firm and steadfast.*
                                    (1 Peter 5:10)

Did you see it? Who will do the restoring? You? Me? No. The God of all grace will restore you. This is better than Chip, Joanna, Bob Vila, or insert the latest TV star carpenter. Your restorer is the God of all grace!

After talking with Barbara about the inside of her house, I consulted with the director of our program. He had seen situations like this before. We called in the big guns. After finishing our workday with the teenagers, we brought in the night shift—a crew to work on the inside of her house. For over a week we just cleaned it out. Trailer after trailer after trailer was filled to the brim. And it was hard—not so much the work as the feelings. I hadn't realized how emotional it would be to carry out Barbara's ruined possessions. She cried; I did too.

Engineers determined that the whole subfloor and joists had to come out and be replaced. They were rotting under the effects of moisture and buckling under the weight of all the stuff. It was a major project. It was not DIY.

After the cleanup work, I stopped going inside the house because it was past my expertise as a sophomore psychology major. Instead, I talked to Barbara. I brought her a photo I'd found in the debris and asked her about some of the people in it. I learned that her son had died in a warehouse accident some years before. As is the case with many of us who hoard in different ways, a traumatic loss had triggered her need to hold on to other things. Barbara told me she hadn't been able to throw out anything since then. She cried some more.

And so we began helping Barbara get the interior work that she needed—not on the ranch-style house, but on the spiritual house. It turned out that the messy house was an expression of her own messiness, and the house's restoration became a sign of the renovation going on inside of her. And it was not DIY. (Have I mentioned that?) As Peter wrote, it was the God of all grace who called her to his eternal glory in Christ, after she had suffered a little while. It was God who would restore her and make her strong, firm, and steadfast.

What Does Renovation Look Like?

Renovation is about seeing yourself as a fixer-upper. But what does it look like?

Its foundation is Jesus.

Immediately following Paul's description in First Corinthians of us as God's building, he writes, "No one can lay any foundation other than the one already laid, which is Jesus Christ" (1 Corinthians 3:11).

To start renovation, oftentimes you have to go all the way down to the foundation. Our damage, like Barbara's, may have been caused by grief and trauma, by the weight of all our stuff. If the foundation was not laid on Jesus, then you may have some work to do. This takes time, but the foundation has to be right.

As I have said, this book will take us on a journey through the Book of Nehemiah. This is an Old Testament story in which you will find no mention of Jesus. No worries. Nehemiah's story is fixed perfectly in the story of God's people. Without mentioning Jesus, the story points to the ultimate hope we as Christians find in him. The longing, and waiting, and building that God's people do in Nehemiah are a precursor to how these things ultimately will be fulfilled by the boy who grows up in Nazareth. As we walk through Nehemiah's story, we will see signposts to the renovation work that only Jesus can do. Even as Nehemiah begins to rebuild Jerusalem, we see how Jesus is at the foundation of it all.

It looks strong.

God will restore you and make you strong, firm, and steadfast. But how many of us right now are feeling strong, firm, and steadfast?

I asked this question of my congregation recently during a worship service. I love my church. They are a group of gifted people who are totally devoted to helping others experience connection in Christ. But when I posed the question and asked for a show of hands, it was clear that they were not feeling strong, firm, and steadfast.

I followed up with another question: "How many of us are feeling anxious, concerned, and easily swayed?" Heads nodded, and hands were raised. Even for those of us who seek to follow faithfully, at times we don't feel very strong. My hope is that as we open ourselves up to a renovation work of God's spirit, we will more fully live into some of the promises God gives us. Sure, there will be times when we are anxious and feel swayed by the wind. But the promise of a renovated life that is strong, firm, and steadfast? I'm ready for that!

It is different.

A renovation looks different from what came before. Same foundation, but it looks starkly different.

My parents just did a big renovation in their house, the house I grew up in. They took out a big wall. The floor was totally refinished, and a new floor was put in to match the old. What I noticed most, though, was that my old bedroom was turned into a music room for my dad's instruments. A wall on one side was taken out, and now a piano is there.

The place looks nothing like when I lived there. I figure this means I can't come back. But I shouldn't have been surprised; a renovation is by nature different. It is exciting, maybe scary while the process is underway, because we don't know exactly how it will look until it is finished.

It is beautiful.

God wants to make something beautiful of your life—not only order out of the mess, but something that looks good! What God wants to do in you is more than cleaning up; it is about a new identity. It is about knowing that you are God's, and that is a beautiful thing.

> *It's in Christ that we find out who we are and*
> *what we are living for. Long before we first heard*

*of Christ and got our hopes up, he had his eye
on us, had designs on us for glorious living,
part of the overall purpose he is working out in
everything and everyone.*
(Ephesians 1:11-12 MSG)

In Christ we find out who we are—this is our identity. And we find out what we are living for—this is our purpose. And both our identity and purpose, in Christ, are beautiful.

Some years ago I sat across the table from one of my mentors, Jorge Acevedo. Jorge is a pastor in Cape Coral, Florida, who has given his life to seeing people changed by connecting with Jesus Christ. He said to a small group of us, "Remember that every person you encounter, every day, is a COGPOW." I had no idea what he was talking about. Everyone else nodded along. I nodded too. I searched my brain. Was this some Greek word I never learned in seminary? Jorge spelled it out for us: "A COGPOW is a Child of God and a Person of Worth." Oh, that COGPOW!

Jorge was right. You are a child of God and a person of worth. In Christ, you are strong; you can be different than you are; and, whether you want to admit it or not, you are beautiful. For many of us, in order to start a renovation with God we will need to affirm that we are indeed of worth. We are of worth to God, which makes us worth the work that God wants to do in us.

One of the things that Andrew and Barbara had to know was that no matter what had come before, nothing had changed their core identity as children of God and persons of worth. No tragedy, no mess, no history can change that. Do you truly believe you are a person of worth? Do you find your key identity in the fact that you are a child of God?

It requires care.

When Paul describes us as God's buildings, he also says this: "Each one should build with care" (1 Corinthians 3:10). God does renovations in us with care, and in the same way we should show care to ourselves.

Renovation is a process. It is not instantaneous. It is not a single event. How long will it take? That's easy: longer than you think.

In the renovation of my parent's house, it took longer than they thought it would. They were matching fifty-year-old wood with five-month-old wood. It required care. It required time. It required a careful process. It actually created a big mess before it started to look good. Most of us want something quick. We want one episode. That's not what we are talking about here. We are opening ourselves up to a lifetime renovation with a God of grace who will restore us. And we won't let a messy inside keep us from letting anyone in, including God.

Never Too Late

It's never too late for a renovation.

Like never.

Last year, in our new church that had started in an elementary school and was meeting in a middle school gym at the time, I saw someone walk in the back during a service. He was wearing shorts, a T-shirt, and a ball cap. No, it wasn't my old friend Andrew (who, by the way, is an officer in the Air Force now!). It was some other dude who dressed like my old friend Andrew.

At our new church, where our main purpose is reaching those who feel disconnected from God, a guy in a hat and shorts is not out of the ordinary. But ever since Andrew, I've learned to pay close attention to these guys. Anyway, the guy walked into our church and sat in the back row. During the last song, he didn't slip out the back. Instead, he walked up front straight to me.

I recognized his face. His name is Stephen. I'd first met him when we were both much younger. We embraced and sat down on the bleachers. Stephen told me that the night before, he had been out late at a bar, drinking. In fact, he had been drinking way too much for way too long. He said that something inside of him had told him he needed to be in church the next morning. He really had never gone to church. So he had scraped himself out of bed that morning and found his way to our church in the middle school gym.

Stephen came back the next week. And the next. And the next. Six months later, on the Sunday after Christmas, he and his teenage son were baptized in a cattle trough in a musty old gymnasium.

A few weeks ago, Stephen celebrated one year of coming to our church and one year of sobriety. He works third shift and raises two kids as a single dad. His life is not easy. But he heard God speak, and he had a breakdown, and he is on a renovation journey the likes of which I have never seen.

All of us, like Stephen, need a renovation.

Are you ready?

Maybe things are really messy inside.

Maybe it would be embarrassing to expose the mess. Certainly easier to keep the door closed.

Maybe you don't know where to start.

Maybe you're like I was and have become so religious that you've forgotten how exciting it is to watch Jesus do what he came to do.

I can't wait to introduce you to this guy I met in 2007. His name is Nehemiah.

And as Nehemiah will show us, it is never too late for a renovation.

2.

Crying and Building

2. CRYING AND BUILDING

When I heard these things, I sat down and wept.
For some days I mourned and fasted and prayed
before the God of heaven.

(Nehemiah 1:4)

Well, I thought I had made it.

It was the first day of school, which in our house is the real start of a new year. Lots of energy, lots of anticipation, lots of anxiety, and lots of good intentions about what lies ahead. And...I thought I had made it.

I mean, we had done the whole deal. My three daughters got up early with butterflies in their stomachs and commitment in their preparation. Each of them donned a new outfit bought by Nana. We took their picture on the front porch as is our tradition (backpacks on with our golden retriever, Zeke, by their side). We successfully posted the pic to social media, and we were off.

We held hands and prayed in the car line.

Our fifth-grader walked in the door with confidence for her sixth and final year in elementary school. She knew, and we knew, she was going to rule that place.

Our six-year-old required a walk-in. I held her hand through the swarm of students in the hallway. Her tummy was turning, and my tummy was turning. We arrived at Ms. Pillow's first-grade classroom, and she went right in and sat down. I took a deep breath.

Then it was off to middle school. The same middle school I had attended twenty-five years ago. The same middle school where our church had worshiped for five years. It was in the parking lot there, a place I had been hundreds of times before, that I noticed the tears. They were sitting right on the edge of my eyes. I had a choice. I could suck them back and be strong, or let them flow and be a blubbering, crying embarrassment to a twelve-year-old. I knew there was no in-between. It was either push them back or this is going to be ugly; like full-on snot and stuff.

I pushed them back. My oldest daughter walked in, definitely not wanting a walk-in. I left the parking lot. I was tough. I thought I had made it. And then, I sat down for a quiet moment to pray and reflect. I opened up my Bible. I was reading Nehemiah. In a quiet moment with another deep breath, the floodgates opened. Tears started flowing. I couldn't stop them. You know, all the life tears.

My girls are getting bigger.

I'm getting older.

Life is sweet; life is precious. Life is hard.

It wasn't just about school drop off at this point. Some of my friends had just received some really good news that week; another set of friends had received devastating news. Same week. Same life.

I'm tired, I realized.

I'm more tired than I've ever been.

I'm not sure if the tears were of relief, grief, pride, or joy. I couldn't make the distinction. But I cried. In Starbucks.

I want to tell you a story in which someone cried. Really cried. And then out of the tears and through the tears, he began to see the sketch of a renovation project. There was a vision of a renovation that God was calling him to that he could never have seen without a big, crying breakdown.

Nehemiah. His name means "comforted by the Lord." But his story does not begin with comfort. It begins with unrest, agitation, and—oh, yes—tears.

It Changed in a Day

Nehemiah lived in a time of great division among his people. The emotions were not unlike what many have experienced recently in the United States. It was a time when very little could be agreed on. As in our own day, if there was one thing the people could all agree on, it was that they didn't agree.

But it wasn't just emotional and relational division. It was also, for many people, a time of true physical displacement and division. The Jews, Nehemiah's people, had been conquered by another empire. They were now ruled by a different king. Many of the Jewish people had been taken from their homes. The

Persians had taken over, had taken the Jews from their home—namely Jerusalem—and had scattered them about. The people identified as gifted and skilled were put into positions all around the region where their gifts and skills could be used for the furtherance of the empire.

Nehemiah was one of these "chosen ones." He had been uprooted from the homeland of his ancestors and sent hundreds of miles away to live in a bustling metropolis among people of a different culture, ethnicity, and religion. Nehemiah was living and working in the Persian city of Susa.

There he was cupbearer to the king.

If it sounds like a menial job, it was not.

Being cupbearer to King Artaxerxes meant, yes, that he brought drinks to the king. It meant that from time to time he would first taste the contents of the cup to make sure it wasn't poisoned. But the cupbearer was also a kind of right-hand person to the king. He was someone who was always close by. He served. He listened. No doubt, he offered counsel. The story, as told in the Bible, seems to insinuate that he was trusted and certainly valued. As a foreigner and a servant, Nehemiah had risen to a high position. Life was not perfect for the people of God, but Nehemiah had done well for himself. For all we know, Nehemiah was comfortable. He was watching his kids grow; he was planning for retirement.

And then, as can happen to any of us, in one day it all changed. His ability to be comfortable, his capacity for contentment went out the window in one conversation.

It happened on the day that Hanani arrived in Susa. Nehemiah describes Hanani as "one of his brothers." Most likely this meant that he was one of Nehemiah's countrymen, a part of his extended family, a fellow Jew. Hanani had come to Susa with a few other people on official business. Nehemiah asked Hanani the obvious question, the question you or I might have asked:

"How are things in Jerusalem?"

Nehemiah was asking, "How is the city? How are our people?" After all, Jerusalem had been the center of Jewish life historically, culturally, and spiritually. Jerusalem was the chosen place for the Temple. Jerusalem was where symbolically—and even in some ways for them literally—God resided.

Jerusalem was strong. It symbolized the strength of the people and the strength of their God. A mighty wall surrounded the city. The wall, maybe more than anything, represented their heritage of provision and protection. The wall was a sign that God had brought them through and would hold them in.

For Jews, most things that were beautiful and important had happened in Jerusalem. Well, at least until this exile. This exile had changed everything.

"How is the city?" asked Nehemiah. "How are our people?"

Hanani answered, "Those who survived the exile and are back in the province are in great trouble and disgrace. The wall of Jerusalem is broken down, and its gates have been burned with fire" (Nehemiah 1:3).

When Nehemiah heard this, his eyes filled with tears. Emotions that he had pushed down began to surface. What feelings were they? Grief, sadness, anger? It was hard to tell. He had a choice. He could choke them back or let them flow.

The Scripture tells us that when Nehemiah heard about the broken wall of Jerusalem, his heart broke, too—the gates now rubble from arson, the city of God in ruins, the people in disgrace. Nehemiah let his feelings flow. He sat down and cried.

For some days, the Bible tells us, he mourned and fasted and prayed.

Nehemiah had risen through the ranks. There were many good things happening in his life. He had steady work. There were parts of his job that were important even. Some parts that he liked. The bills were being paid. He should have been fine just to push through and move on. But one mention of brokenness in his family, his people, his nation, and Nehemiah was on the floor, crying.

Nehemiah was no longer content.

He felt that he was supposed to be doing something else. He knew it. There was a greater work yet to be done, and he was supposed to do it. (You can nod along if this connects.)

Nehemiah knew that a renovation project was needed, and he had a sneaking suspicion that it would involve him in a big way.

The story of Nehemiah is an amazing account of daring, courage, hard work, and opposition. It describes the restoration of a city, of a nation, and of a man.

And it all started with tears.

Renovation starts with tears (almost every time).

Yep, almost every time when there is a beautiful renovation, if you can trace it back to the beginning you will find mourning, praying, and crying.

A Season of Grief

When my wife, Rachel, and I left Atlanta in 2007, we moved back to our hometown to start a new church. We could not have been more excited about the work before us, but we also had to do all the things people do when moving to a new place.

It started with finding a place to live. When we first saw the home we would eventually buy, it was still under—you guessed it—renovation. What had been a thousand-square-foot log cabin was being added on to. A garage, a master bedroom, dining and laundry rooms with all-new features were being added to the place. It was pretty cool. It had some old and some new. Most of the cabin still had decades-old logs visible on the inside.

Our trusted real estate agent strongly discouraged us from buying it. Her experience told her that a lot of things we couldn't see might be problematic. There could be hidden costs. That particular house, in her opinion, was not the right buy for us at that particular time.

She asked us to think about it, but I didn't have to. After one look, I was all in.

Even though the cabin needed months of work, I saw what it could be. The unknown excited me. We bought it before the work was done. We moved in with my parents and we waited. We waited and we waited. Then finally, after months of bunking with the folks, the house was done, and our family moved into our new old cabin. Our fixer-upper.

Life was grand. And then—as can happen to any of us, as Nehemiah discovered—it changed in a moment. Two weeks into cabin living, I noticed a wet spot on the bathroom wall. It was in an area that had been renovated. The next day the spot was bigger. On the third day, water bubbled through the surface of the wall. I called a plumber. After a quick investigation, he informed me that when the bathroom had been restored; one small nail had gone into a water pipe behind the wall. One measly nail. Water had been flowing inside the walls for weeks before it showed on the outside. Interior studs and drywall were soaked. Mold had set in.

It was too late to patch it. Everything had to come out. A demolition crew came into my new old cabin that had just been fully renovated and, wearing masks, began tearing it up and tearing it out.

Wheelbarrows rolled in and out for two days. The fixtures we had picked out, the tile we had chosen, the carpet with the color we loved were all carried out to a dumpster.

We cried.

For some days.

We had to rebuild again.

Make no mistake, Nehemiah had a breakdown. That's what crying for some days is called. You may be in such a season right now. A season of grief. A season of tears.

Can you relate to Nehemiah? You were just doing your thing, and then in a moment everything changed. Maybe it was a phone call or a medical test. Maybe it was a relationship that you cherished or a loved one who suddenly was gone. Or maybe it was slower for you. Perhaps you didn't notice how tired you were becoming. It slipped up on you. But you felt the tears. They were right there on the surface. Like me, maybe you had a choice. You could choke them back or let them flow. That's when renovation happens.

We don't renovate when everything is OK, when we are content with things. A rebuild starts with tears almost every time. If you are looking at a mess right now; if you have been brought to your knees; if you feel the tears...then you are primed for renovation.

Saying No

Nehemiah heard about the condition of Jerusalem. Jerusalem was in disgrace, and if Jerusalem was in disgrace, it meant his people were in disgrace. He was in disgrace. Even though he had a good income and food on his table, all was not well. Nehemiah cried. For some days he mourned and fasted and prayed.

And then he said no.

"No" meant "I'm not content with this."

"No" meant "This is not going to cut it."

"No" meant "I need to do something."

Tanna Clark said no. Tanna was a stay-at-home mom in our neighborhood. We went to church together and were in a small group together. And then, in a moment, everything changed for Tanna. She went on a short-term mission trip to Haiti with an organization called Soles4Souls, which collects and distributes shoes and clothing. What Tanna saw in Haiti made Tanna cry. For some days. She saw some things that made her think, "This isn't going to cut it." It didn't happen quickly, but over a period of years she formed a nonprofit organization that built a school and that now feeds and educates hundreds of kids a day. It started with no.

Ingrid was my friend growing up. Like me, she went to seminary after college. Like me, she took the classes to become a United Methodist pastor. Like me, she returned home to the Nashville area after finishing school. There, she saw hundreds of people living on the streets. She cried. A bunch. Then she said, "No, that's not going to cut it." Ingrid could have been the pastor of many churches in our area, but instead she began living and working among those who live and work on the streets. Her church is in the streets. There is no building. It's the people of the streets. She began to help them get out of the cold. Then she began to help them find permanent housing. She is now building a village made up of "micro-homes"—houses of less than 500 square feet—as a bridge to permanent housing for the people of her church. It's a big renovation project, but Ingrid was not content with the alternative.

Stephen, whom you met in chapter 1, had gone through a particularly bad season, and really a particularly bad night. In the depths of that season, he cried his eyes out and said no to drunkenness. Saying no led to a remarkable renovation that was witnessed by our entire church. We celebrated his first-year anniversary of sobriety with a standing ovation. To get to that ovation, there was intentionality and there were lots of steps. But it started with no. It started with "This isn't going to cut it anymore."

Saying Yes

After saying no, we can say yes to a renovation. We don't see it explicitly in Nehemiah's opening chapter, because it takes some time for him to say the yes out loud. But I'm certain that Nehemiah, in his heart, resolved an emphatic yes and decided to leave what was comfortable and go back to rebuild the mess. Something had happened in the tears that allowed Nehemiah to see an alternative to brokenness. Somewhere in the breakdown, he began to get a glimpse of a different future.

In First Peter, we are told that "you also, like living stones, are being built into a spiritual house" (1 Peter 2:5a). I believe God gives us this image of a house as a way of helping us understand how we can be rebuilt and renovated. I acknowledge that if I am a house, I am a fixer-upper. I may be habitable, but everyone knows I am in need of some work.

But I also claim that it is never too late for a renovation. In that claim, I begin to say yes to the vision God has for me. I squint my eyes and try to see that vision of a new reality coming from my current mess.

One of the things I love about do-it-yourself shows on TV is that they show you a sketch. Often they show you the old, run-down house and superimpose a sketch of what the renovated house will look like. You're standing in the old living room with the outdated paneling and shag carpeting, but because of the sketch we are able to glimpse what it will look like with new lighting and shiplap (there's always shiplap). The sketch doesn't show exactly what the place will look like, but it's close enough to get you dreaming and working. It's enough to move you forward.

Being Honest

Restoration requires honesty. In Nehemiah's prayer, he came before God and was brutally honest.

*"I confess the sins we Israelites, including myself
and my father's family, have committed against
you. We have acted very wickedly toward you.
We have not obeyed the commands, decrees and
laws you gave your servant Moses."*
(Nehemiah 1:6b-7)

That, my friends, is holding nothing back.

Nehemiah understood the mess and how the Israelites got there. He understood his part in the mess and owned it. He was real about where they were and what needed to be done to move forward. You can't do major renovation without being honest about the mess and honest about how hard it will be to change it.

When our cabin was in a mess, I had just moved from one city to another for the express purpose of doing something that I had no idea how to do. I was supposed to be starting a new church. That alone was a big project. That should have been my main focus. Instead, I was living in a renovated cabin that was a financial stretch to buy in the first place, and it mocked me every morning and evening.

A part of tearing everything out of the house included taking the fixtures that could be salvaged and setting them on the porch that faced the road. They put our toilet out on the porch. There was a window in our bedroom where I could see it when I lay in bed. Every night I fell asleep to the toilet, and every morning I woke up to the sunrise glimmering off the porcelain. If by chance I ever forgot that everything was a mess, if for a moment I thought I had things under control, the old toilet sitting on my porch would say, "Not so fast, buckaroo."

The story of Nehemiah shows us that some deep, important work can happen when you can no longer hide just how bad things are. Thanks to that toilet, it was as if I was calling out to my neighbors, "Hey, look what I've got on the porch! Everything is not great in here! We're having a tough time! We actually don't have the money to renovate again! We are fighting it out with the builder! It's causing a lot of stress in our marriage! I'm supposed to be killing it at my job right now, but I feel like my job is killing me!" I figured with the toilet out there, I might as well just go ahead and be honest about it.

It may sound crazy, but that kind of honesty, the you-can't-hide-it-anymore kind of honesty, is precisely where God can make something beautiful. It's in that place of honest brokenness that we remember and see the promises of God.

Nehemiah teaches us the next step, and it's a surprising one: We are to remind God of God's promises.

Check this out. After Nehemiah was brutally honest about his part in the mess, he told God,

> *"Remember the instruction you gave your*
> *servant Moses, saying, 'If you are unfaithful, I*
> *will scatter you among the nations, but if you*
> *return to me and obey my commands, then even*
> *if your exiled people are at the farthest horizon,*
> *I will gather them from there and bring them to*
> *the place I have chosen as a dwelling for*
> *my Name.'"*
>
> *(Nehemiah 1:8-9)*

Now, do we really think God needed to be reminded of God's promises? Do we think God forgot what God said? No.

Who needed to be reminded? Nehemiah.

What if we tried that?

God, you said you would never leave me. God, you said that no matter what I go through you wouldn't tempt me beyond what I can bear. God, you said that I was of great value to you, that even if I was in the biggest mess you would come after me. God, you said your grace was sufficient for all my messes, that in my weakness your strength is made perfect. God, you called Nehemiah to a time of crying and praying. Well, that's where I am. But you led him back and he did restore the city. The wall was rebuilt. The people worshiped again. The poor were taken care of and fed. Remember that, God? Remember?

I think God might be, like, "Yeah, I remember. Do you?"

As we remind God of God's promises, we begin to glimpse the sketch again. We don't fully see what it will be, but we see enough. We remember that this is not DIY. There is no do-it-yourself here.

This is something that God and only God can do. God will do the renovation. God "will himself restore you and make you strong, firm and steadfast" (1 Peter 5:10). Not you—God.

Questions to Ponder

When you're planning a renovation, it might be worth making some space in your heart and life to ponder some questions.

What puts tears in the corners of your eyes?

For some of us, the tears come from relationship. Maybe, like Nehemiah, they come from acknowledging the brokenness in our family. Maybe they come from a loss, an illness, a death, a regret—all of these can do it. There are many things, and it is usually not one thing.

It doesn't have to be a bad thing, either. The natural passage of time and even expected transitions can put us on our knees. When I cried on the first day of school, it was from something that was hard to put into words. There was loss but also joy.

What has put you on the verge of tears? Are you willing to let them fall?

What do you need to say no to?

Sometimes tears show us things in our lives to which we should say no. Granted, many things that make us cry are beyond our control and just need to be grieved and cried about. Other things, however, are in our control—things that God can make strong, firm, and steadfast; but first we need to say, "Not going to happen anymore."

I'm reminded of three questions we answer in our baptisms. Perhaps the most memorable part is often called the Profession of Faith, when we are asked this question: "Do you confess Jesus Christ as your Savior, put your whole trust in his grace, and promise to serve him as your Lord?"

Sometimes, though, we overlook the two questions that come before the Profession of Faith. You forgot them, didn't you?

The first question is called the Renunciation of Sin. A renunciation is a rejection. It is saying a big fat no. Here's the first question: "Do you renounce the spiritual forces of wickedness, reject the evil powers of this world, and repent of your sin?"

We say, "I do." But really we are saying no—no to wickedness, no to evil powers, and no to sin.

I wouldn't want to rank the three questions; they are all essential. You need all three, but the next question, the second one—well, don't miss it. Here's the second question: "Do you accept the freedom and power God gives you to resist evil, injustice, and oppression in whatever forms they present themselves?"

If the first question is a big fat no, this is one is a huge yes. Yes, God. Having said no to the reality of sin and evil power, we say yes to a God who gives power. A God who will restore.

It is then and only then that we can profess our faith and confess Jesus Christ as Lord and Savior.

What does the sketch look like?

Thinking back to the sketch of your renovation, what does it look like for you? What is God calling you to be, to experience, to do? When I say no, what am I saying yes to?

Nehemiah saw rebuilt walls and the Temple full of worshipers. What do you see? When you wipe the tears away, what renovation sketch is God placing in your heart?

Sometimes the tears have clouded our vision too much, and we need someone else to help us see it.

Standing on the porch of our cabin, one of the workers said to me, "This is going to look better than ever when we're finished." We were standing next to a toilet at the time.

OK, maybe that's a bad example. Let's be done with the toilet. The point is, when you face renovation, make sure you don't go it alone. More on this later, but you will need others to help you see and believe in the sketch.

What do you need to be honest about?

A part of Nehemiah's honesty was acknowledging and articulating his own role in the mess. If you don't claim your role, you won't be able to move forward. Be honest with God; be honest with others. Stop playing. Stop pretending.

And then, in that honest, broken place, you can begin the fun part: reminding the all-knowing God of things God already remembers.

What do you need to remind God of, so you can remind yourself?

I listed some of these reminders earlier. But here's my biggest one: God, you said I don't have to be afraid.

Among the Bible's many renovation projects, this is perhaps God's most repeated promise. We read it over and over again: Do not be afraid. Do not fear. Be strong and courageous.

This is God's promise when you need renovation. It's scary to take all the clutter out of your living room. Who doesn't get shaky knees when you start tearing out a wall? It's terrifying to make a bigger mess after cleaning up the first mess.

So try it: Remind God what God has said over and over again. The repetition seems to please God, and I promise it can calm a worried heart.

*   *   *

In a weird way, these questions remind me of what happened on back-to-school day. As a dad, I cried as I thought about all I wanted to be for my daughters and all I was not. Doing so made me lean that much harder on the One who could make things strong, firm, and steadfast.

On that first day of school, I saw the sketch. It was part of why I was crying. Back-to-school day was when I noticed how my daughters had grown. When I compared this year's photo with the one from last year, I realized that we weren't where we were before. But that was all part of the vision. That was all a part of the hope that things would indeed change. My girls would grow and mature and be beautiful. I cried because I have an untouchable hope that God's plan for the future is good and worth pushing forward for.

I believe it for the three girls who are growing up with the golden retriever, as I believe it for the kids at Tanna's school in Haiti, as I believe it for Ingrid's church members on the streets, as I believe it for my friend Stephen. As God believes it for you. God has a design in mind. God has a renovation plan.

And it starts with tears. Almost every time.

3.

What to Know
Before You Build

3. WHAT TO KNOW BEFORE YOU BUILD

I said to them, "You see the trouble we are in: Jerusalem lies in ruins, and its gates have been burned with fire. Come, let us rebuild the wall of Jerusalem, and we will no longer be in disgrace." I also told them about the gracious hand of my God on me and what the king had said to me.

They replied, "Let us start rebuilding." So they began this good work.

(Nehemiah 2:17-18)

You are probably familiar with one of the most classic children's games of all time, a wonderful time-tested game of energy, intrigue, and deception. It requires no accessories and no board. The rules are easy to learn and can be adapted to almost any setting.

I'm talking about hide-and-seek.

Hide-and-seek is the oldest game in the book. Literally. It began with Adam and Eve in the garden of Eden. Abraham played it. Moses was a master. David was one of the best. Jonah, a champion. Well, for a while. Your grandparents played it. I saw it being played in a remote village in Nicaragua. You can see it played every day on inner-city streets, playgrounds, and wooded backyards.

I play hide-and-seek with a six-year-old who doesn't want to be found. The only problem is, she is really terrible at hiding. When she hides, you can still see her. A leg sticks out from behind a tree. A ribbon shows above the shrubs. She crouches behind a couch, but her closed eyes don't hide the fact that her whole body is clearly in the open.

"All right! I'm ready!" she calls out, her voice directing me exactly where to go. And there she hides, like an ostrich with her head in the sand.

And what do I do? Pretend I don't see her, of course.

"Where's Phoebe?" I call out. "Has anyone seen Phoebe?"

Usually one of her older sisters will say, "Yeah, Dad, she's right there," ruining the game. Big sisters don't always know how to play along.

I've heard people use hide-and-seek as a way of describing how we try to avoid God. Like Phoebe, we hide from God, but we really don't.

However, that's not what I want us to focus on here. I want to think about the other side of that coin—the times when it feels like God is hiding from us.

Let's go back to my game of hide-and-seek with Phoebe, this time when she is seeking and I'm hiding. Do you know what I do? I run fast and far to a place I think she would never look. I'm an adult with over thirty years of hide-and-seek experience. I know how to conceal myself perfectly. So I hide in a closet, around a corner, behind a door. I hear her call, "Ready or not, here I come!" I don't breathe. She searches and searches, but she can't find me. Then I hear her calling out for me. "Where are you, Dad? I can't find you!" I sit like a statue. I hear her begin to cry. "Where are you, Daddy? I'm done with the game. Just come out!" But no, I'm committed to the game. Eventually she gives up. She gives up on the game, she gives up on me, and I win.

That's what I do, right?

No!

It's cruel. It's ugly. Just the fact that I would make up such a story has some of you wondering what kind of person I am. Who would do such a thing? No good parent, that's for sure.

God wouldn't do it either.

And yet, sometimes when we talk about God, wondering where we're supposed to go and what we're supposed to do, the God we imagine seems to be playing hide-and-seek like the bad dad in my story.

Looking back on it, that's what Rachel and I felt when we heard the question, "Will you go wherever I want you to go?" You see, we had our plan. We liked to think we would go where God wanted us to go, but truthfully we were expecting God to conform to our plan, the one we had laid out so clearly. After all, we had gone over it with God numerous times. But God wasn't talking about our plan. God was asking if we would conform our lives to the Spirit's leading. That was a whole different thing, because I was used to leading.

Finally, we relented. We submitted. On our knees, with tears in our eyes, we said, "OK, God we will go wherever you want us to go."

And we waited. We waited for God to tell us—you know, tell us where God wanted us to go. But I heard no voices. No writing appeared on the wall. Either one of those would have been really helpful. I even imagined what it would look like if God drew an arrow on the floor. But God didn't. And I had no idea what to do.

One day over coffee with a trusted friend, I laid out my predicament. I told him how we had submitted. I told him how we would go wherever God wanted, no strings attached. I told him how we were agonizing over this. The louder we called out to God, it seemed the quieter God got.

My friend looked me in the eye, and I'll never forget what he said. His words forever changed the way I would think about God's call and our response.

He said, "It sounds like you think God is playing hide-and-seek with you. Is that what you think?"

I answered honestly, "Well, yeah, I hadn't thought about it like that, but it kind of feels that way."

Where are you, God? I'm done with the game. Just come out!

My friend said, "God doesn't play hide-and-seek like that, Jacob, not the way you're describing."

You and I can't conceive of a dad who would hide from his little girl until she was in tears and gave up on the game. And I urge you not to conceive of a God who would do that to you. I urge you not to conceive of a God who would call you to a big work, a renovation, a rebuild of your spiritual house, then leave you alone and hide in the closet. If you've been taught that God is like that, or if you've been shown that God could do those things, I urge you to believe in a God who is different. A God who is good. Really good. I urge you to believe in a God who won't leave you hanging.

I pray that we hear in Nehemiah's story how, even though the journey is difficult and God seems quiet at times, there is always a way forward. We just need to know a few things before we build.

Nehemiah's Restoration Project

Remember when Nehemiah cried after hearing the condition of Jerusalem? The walls were torn down, the gates burned, the Temple no longer a holy place of worship.

It broke his heart.

Nehemiah cried. He was honest. He reminded God of God's promises. Then he went to the king.

Keep in mind that this was the same king of the same empire that had conquered Nehemiah's people. Nehemiah went to that king and asked permission to go back and rebuild something that had been torn down.

And the king said yes!

God was giving Nehemiah a break.

Nehemiah leaped into action. He returned to Jerusalem, excited to begin the restoration project—excited or afraid, it was hard to tell. Here is what he tells us:

> *I went to Jerusalem, and after staying there*
> *three days I set out during the night with a few*
> *others. I had not told anyone what my God had*
> *put in my heart to do for Jerusalem.*
>
> *(Nehemiah 2:11-12b)*

Did you catch that? It was three days before he could muster the courage even to look around. Then when he did go to look, he went in the middle of the night so no one would know. He took some others with him, but he didn't tell them what they were looking for!

In the darkness, torch in hand, he examined the burned gates of his beloved city. He saw that the walls had been torn down. What he had been told in Susa was true. The strength of God's city—real and symbolic—was no more.

Nighttime mission under his belt, mind spinning with all that needed to be done, his heart overwhelmed with emotion, and *still* he told no one. He hadn't told anyone what he was doing!

> *The officials did not know where I had gone*
> *or what I was doing, because as yet I had said*
> *nothing to the Jews or the priests or nobles or*
> *officials or any others who would be doing the*
> *work.*
>
> *(Nehemiah 2:16)*

I'm so glad this part of Nehemiah's story wasn't left out. I'm so glad we didn't just get "Nehemiah heard from God and then went back and rebuilt Jerusalem." That statement would have been true, but we would have missed the season we all go through before we do anything. We would have missed what we need to know before we rebuild.

Yes, Nehemiah had a powerful moment and was called to rebuild. We see that the call to rebuild Jerusalem, though, was not just about bricks and mortar. This was also about renovating Nehemiah. And right after Nehemiah accepted the call, everything got messy and scary. It was unclear what he was supposed to do or what God was telling him. He was afraid. He floundered. He took midnight recon missions. I wonder if it felt like God was playing hide-and-seek.

If you find yourself in the season before the action, if you feel God calling you to something but aren't sure what do to do or when to do it, then pay attention to the first two chapters of Nehemiah. If you have said no to the current reality and yes to a rebuild, then check out what came next for Nehemiah: crying, mourning, fasting, praying, asking, planning, and examining— days, maybe weeks, perhaps months of it. *And* he didn't tell anybody.

Do you have something in your heart right now that you have been crying over, mourning over, praying and planning over? Do you have something like that, and you have yet to tell anyone? Then check out what Nehemiah did next.

Finally, finally, finally after all that, after examining the city in the middle of the night, finally Nehemiah told somebody.

> *I said to them, "You see the trouble we are in:*
> *Jerusalem lies in ruins, and its gates have been*
> *burned with fire. Come, let us rebuild the wall of*
> *Jerusalem, and we will no longer be in disgrace."*
> *I also told them about the gracious hand of my*
> *God on me and what the king had said to me.*
> (Nehemiah 2:17-18a)

He finally let it all out. He just gushed the story. He told of the call, the crying, and the prayer. He told them about the king saying yes! He told them about what God had put on his heart. And do you know what the people said?

"Let us start rebuilding" (v. 18b).

Yep, that's what they said. Let's do it. We're in. We believe. We are with you.

Wow. After all the internal processing, after wondering what people would say, after I'm sure his fair share of doubt, Nehemiah told the people about his crazy dream of renovation and they said, "Let us start rebuilding."

Another Restoration Project

My own wrestling match with God had led me from Atlanta back to my hometown to start a church. (With a name like Jacob, I guess I should have given more thought to what can happen when you wrestle with God.) It didn't, however, lead me to start the church immediately. It took weeks and months of praying and examining, during which I was filled with excitement and almost crippling fear.

I found, though, that God had given me favor, and in fact God had been preparing things long before I got there. For example, I didn't need to hone my skills as a convincing salesman (skills I did not have). Instead, I needed to practice telling my story—the story of how God had called me. What I found were people who, without me doing a sales pitch, immediately said, "We're in."

Marianne and Pat showed up at one of our first gatherings, held in our home. Marianne and Pat were two of my mom's best friends. I couldn't believe they were there. They had helped raise me. They knew me. And that scared me. I figured my mom had probably asked them to come to make me feel better. Well, it worked. Two people joining the team may seem like a small thing, but their presence was a way of saying, "Let us start rebuilding," and it boosted me.

Then there were Bob and Joan. It had been a couple of years since that early gathering in our home, and we were a church just finding our footing, meeting in Stoner Creek Elementary School. Yes, the name of our meeting place was Stoner Creek. We had a great outreach to recovering hippies. Walking out of Stoner Creek Elementary one Sunday, Bob and Joan asked me if I would visit them that week. Bob and Joan were a couple who had retired to live in a beautiful home near the lake in our community. They had worked long and hard, and now was their time to relax and enjoy the fruits of their labors.

I went to their home the next day. I was greeted with a cup of coffee, and we sat down in their den. They said they had prayed about it and wanted to give a six-figure gift for the building campaign. The thing is, there was no building campaign. There was no sketch. There was only the dream in my heart. But God had been preparing them long before I ever shared it. You can imagine my shock when they told me. There is still a coffee stain on the floor in their den to mark that historic moment.

Fast-forward a few months. We learned that land was available right where we hoped to build the church. We had known it would be expensive. It was. It was the perfect spot, but reluctantly we looked elsewhere.

Two years later, we heard that the land price had been dropped. It was still at least a half million more than we could afford, but we set up a meeting anyway. We met with the landowners in a fancy boardroom on the other side of town. All the business people talked business, but eventually an elderly man at the table asked me to tell him about the church. It turned out he was the principal landowner. I fumbled for words. I hadn't expected to say much at the meeting. I told him about my dream, the call that God had placed on my heart. I told him how Rachel and I were trying to answer a question God had asked us.

We offered them the biggest stretch the church could make: fifty percent less than the original asking price. They said they would return with a counteroffer. The next week they did. They accepted our offer. Stunned, we asked, "Why?" The elderly man told us he believed in the dream.

You Are Not Alone

So often we hold the dream in our heart. We do all the praying, planning, and examining we can do without once sharing what we think God is asking of us. But in doing so, we ignore one of the important truths about renovation. Before you rebuild, you have to tell somebody—tell somebody about the dream God has put into your heart for restoring you, renovating you, and doing the miraculous.

Sometimes this inner struggle causes serious anxiety, and that certainly was the case with me. When I first began to struggle with anxiety—this was in college, years before starting the new church—I would stay up through the night. I would drive until sunrise with shaking hands. I would go to the emergency room alone. For some reason I believed that the struggle was mine alone. It was something I would have to figure out. On. My. Own. I thought healing was possible, but I didn't believe anyone could help me.

One night, though, I was exposed. I got in the car to do my midnight solo drive through the city. I entered the E.R. of the local hospital, filled with fear. I didn't know what was going on. I had not yet learned what a panic attack was. I thought I was dying. I went to a pay phone (remember those?) and called my parents' house. It rang twice and I hung up. Instead of entering the hospital, I walked out and continued my midnight drive, hour after hour.

When I finished my drive the next morning, exhausted, I found out my parents had been frantically searching for me. They had seen the number on caller ID from the hospital in their son's college town, and they weren't giving up until they found me.

I was caught. I told them about my fears and my struggle. I was honest. I needed help. And do you know what they did? They helped. They helped me get help. They helped me get better.

I learned that day that other people struggle. I learned I wasn't alone. I might never have found out if I hadn't shared my deepest feelings. It happened against my will, but I'm so glad it did. God did a renovation in my heart. I still struggle, but I know I'm not alone.

Nehemiah wouldn't tell anyone about the rebuilding project that God had laid on his heart. He thought it was all about him. Even after he went to Jerusalem and got help examining the damage to the city, he didn't tell anyone. Not a soul. Finally, he worked up the courage to say something.

"This is crazy," he said, "but I know for my life to be restored, I have to be a part of rebuilding the city." And they said...

"Let's start rebuilding!"

In that moment, Nehemiah learned that his good Father wasn't playing games with him. It wasn't hide-and-seek. All the praying and examining and planning didn't have to be done alone. It was all a part of God calling him to renovation.

In the next chapter, I'll tell you about all the people who are going to oppose you as you seek to do God's work, the people who will say, "You have to be kidding me." But not here. Put those worries aside for a moment. Right now, focus on telling people what God is stirring in your heart. The risk is worth it. You will find that you are not alone.

Before Rebuilding

If you have a renovation on your heart, share it. Tell a friend. But before you start rebuilding, you should know a few things.

Renovation is hard.

Two of my good friends are builders. When I started working on this book, I texted them both, separately, and asked a question: "What's easier—a renovation project or a new build?"

The first friend answered quickly: "Renovation is always harder. You have to deal with the stuff already there." The other answered soon after: "New build is easier. Remodels have many problems."

The work that God wants us to do is a renovation, a rebuild. It will be hard, it will take time, and it will require care.

God is preparing others too.

This isn't a solo sport. Your personal restoration, the thing God is calling you to, will not be done in isolation. It's exciting to find out who and through whom God has been preparing.

Jesus told the disciples, "I sent you to reap what you have not worked for. Others have done the hard work, and you have reaped the benefits of their labor" (John 4:38).

God's renovation projects always precede us and involve other people. The thing is, we just see a piece at a time. Be assured, though, that the restoration involves more than just you. It's a community project.

Renovation requires faith.

If we understand faith as belief in things we can't see, then renovation is all about faith. On TV, Chip and Joanna ask their clients for faith every time. To renovate, you have to believe in something that you can't yet see, or that you don't see clearly.

> *For now we see through a glass, darkly; but then*
> *face to face: now I know in part; but then shall I*
> *know even as also I am known.*
> *(1 Corinthians 13:12 KJV)*

Renovation is all about God's power.

When you rebuild by yourself—you know, DIY—you get to see how awesome you are. People compliment your hard work and ingenuity. That's fun for a while. But when you rebuild with faith, when you hang in through the praying, planning, and examining, then you get to see God's power magnified.

You'll have questions.

Questions are inevitable. Take some time to ponder before you rebuild.

Are you struggling to know the next step?

Are you trying to see what God is up to?

Where do you need to slow down?

Whom do you need to tell?

* * *

You may have heard all manner of things about God. Some things that you've heard may lead you to feel God is not good.

I get that. But as gently as I can, I want to assure you of some things.

God is good.

God is not playing games with you.

The call you feel to renovation is real.

The hope to change your life is holy.

Change takes patience.

It takes vulnerability.

It takes faith.

It's worth it.

4.

When Others Don't Like Your Plans

4. WHEN OTHERS DON'T LIKE YOUR PLANS

Tobiah the Ammonite, who was at his [Sanballat's] side, said, "What they are building—even a fox climbing up on it would break down their wall of stones!"

(Nehemiah 4:3)

There is a moment for each of us when the lie is sown. It's a part of your story. It's a part of every story. It's right there in the first story.

You've heard it before. Everything is going splendidly in a garden of grace. A craftsman has created perfection. There is no need for a renovation; everything is sparkling new.

That's when the lie is sown. A serpent, described as the most cunning of all creatures, shows up and tells a big fat lie. If the big fat lie is believed, the sparkling new everything gets broken. And, of course, that's exactly what happens.

The serpent asks, "Did God really say you couldn't eat from any tree?" Eve speaks up first and says, "Um, no. God says we can eat from any tree except one."

Saying you can eat from any tree except one is a lot different from saying you can't eat from any tree. So you see how the lie is starting.

Eve says, "If we eat from the one tree, we die." The serpent says, "That's not true. God doesn't want you to eat from that tree because then you will be like God, and God doesn't want that."

Lies can be confusing and multilayered, and Eve finds herself looking at that one tree. Suddenly, believing the lie of the cunning one, she finds that particular tree to be especially enticing. It's the same thing you and I do. Like Eve, we look and see and eat. And usually, like Eve, we pass it around.

The lies today are the same ones that Adam and Eve heard in the garden.

Don't trust God.

You need something more than what God has provided.

God doesn't have your best interests in mind.

The lies lead to insecurity and shame.

Maybe you remember when the lie was sown in your life. Was it from a parent, a teacher, a peer? Was it in the lunchroom, the playground, the living room? That moment when you heard and believed the lie may have led you to a great, great loss. And now your defenses are up, your insecurity is high, and shame runs rampant.

Reading Nehemiah's story, you may be inspired to step out and let God do a renovating work in you. But when you do, make no mistake: you will encounter enemies. If you didn't believe in an enemy before, a cunning serpent who sows lies, you soon will.

I actually don't talk and write about the devil much. I don't like to give him press. I think sometimes we give the devil more credit than he deserves. But if you've opened your heart to a renovation, if you've begun to pray for whatever beautiful thing God wants to do in you, I'm just telling you that you will hear a lie or two.

Sometimes it's the cunning serpent sowing the lie as he did in the perfect garden. Sometimes it's a mean boss; other times it's someone you live with. Sometimes it's an old lie from a long time ago, still rattling around in your head and heart. But you're going to hear a lie or two, and you need to be ready.

The Ongoing Saga of Nehemiah

Remember, Nehemiah finally worked up the courage to tell people that God had called him to a renovation project, the rebuilding of the wall of Jerusalem and the restoration of the people. Remember what they said in response: "Let's start rebuilding!"

Well, they did. The third chapter of Nehemiah tells who joined him and where they began their work. The chapter is really just a long list of all the people who believed in Nehemiah's dream and were ready to jump in.

In the fourth chapter of Nehemiah, the lies start. They show what I have found to be a consistent truth of stepping out to do what God wants. There will be a bunch of people who believe in your dream and want to help. And there will be a handful of people who are just plain mad about it. These are the ones who throw the lies.

In Nehemiah's story, Sanballat was the maddest. Sanballat held some kind of command in Jerusalem. We aren't really sure what his authority was, but he had some. Sanballat was not happy about the servant class mobilizing and rebuilding. He felt threatened by it, probably even a little afraid. He asked,

> *"What are those feeble Jews doing? Will they
> restore their wall? Will they offer sacrifices? Will
> they finish in a day? Can they bring the stones
> back to life from those heaps of rubble—burned
> as they are?"*
>
> (Nehemiah 4:2)

Sanballat, as often happens, had a sidekick. His name was Tobiah, and he chimed in, "even a fox climbing up on it would break down their wall of stones!" (v. 3).

I guess that was the best comment he could come up with on short notice. Good one, Tobiah. I hear Tobiah following up his snappy comment with a maniacal laugh, like all evil sidekicks do.

To me, Tobiah is that kid on the bus who made fun of you. His cut-downs were lame, but somehow they still stung.

"Four-eyes!"

That's what the Tobiah on Bus 129 said to me in 1987 on the first day I wore glasses. Four-eyes. Really? How lame is that? Oldest one in the book. Is that really the best you got? But, of course, it hurt. And I remember it thirty years later.

"Even a fox climbing up on it would break down their wall of stones!"

Sounds just as dumb, right? Who cares? Who was Sanballat anyway? He didn't hold authority over Nehemiah. Nehemiah had written permission from the king. And Tobiah with his lame cut-downs—big deal, right?

Well, for the Jews who had begun the work of rebuilding, it rattled them a bit. They cried out and asked God to take care of it. They shook it off. They heard the opposition, it bothered them, and they moved on.

But the lie was sown.

We've all had a moment like that. Mine came a couple of years before the experience in Atlanta, when I first felt called to start a church. I was twenty-five years old, I was pumped, and I really believed God would do something through me. I went to an older pastor, someone I trusted, and shared the dream. I laid it all out.

The pastor said, "Jacob, you aren't the kind of guy who can start a church." And he explained why. I have to admit, he had some good points.

As I walked out of his office, I kept telling myself, "I don't know about this. It didn't sound like truth." But I was rattled, and during tough times I still think about it. To this day I can list his reasons.

Lies get sown. Sometimes our parents sow them without even knowing it; they had their own lies given to them. Sometimes it's a teacher or a coach or a boss or a spouse. And those lies are hard to shake once they get in there.

Let's stay with Nehemiah a bit longer.

> *We rebuilt the wall till all of it reached half*
> *its height, for the people worked with all their*
> *heart.*
>
> *(v. 6)*

The people were working with all their heart. Sanballat's opposition and Tobiah's cut-downs were not enough to deter them. Did you see it? They rebuilt the wall to half its height!

> *But when Sanballat, Tobiah, the Arabs, the*
> *Ammonites and the people of Ashdod heard that*
> *the repairs to Jerusalem's walls had gone ahead*
> *and that the gaps were being closed, they were*
> *very angry. They all plotted together to come*
> *and fight against Jerusalem and stir up trouble*
> *against it.*
>
> *(vv. 7-8)*

All right, this wasn't just about cut-downs anymore. An army was being gathered to come and take the Jews out.

We've seen that the devil is likely to throw a couple of lies your way when you say, "I want to be restored" or "I want to see something beautiful come out of my mess." But, let's be honest, the enemy has seen you try and fail before, so he's not too concerned. But when you start making progress and the wall is halfway built? That's a different story.

Keep in mind that in this case, "half its height" was nothing to sneeze at. The wall that had been torn down had probably been about 4,000 meters around, with an average height of 12 meters. If you aren't hip to the metric system, that's about 2.5 miles around and in some places 40 feet high. So, in a short time with help of the people listed in Nehemiah 3, the wall had been rebuilt to a height of perhaps 20 feet.

That, friends, is significant progress. Like when you make it a month sober. Like when you and your wife are six months into counseling and you're laughing again. Like when you suffer a terrible loss but have hope again.

With this kind of progress, your enemies will be way past cut-downs; you'd better get ready for a fight.

Nehemiah knew it, too. When the wall was 20 feet high and they were extending the scaffolding to 40 feet, Nehemiah knew they were in for a big fight.

And, oh yeah, one other minor detail: they were dog-tired.

> *Meanwhile, the people in Judah said, "The strength of the laborers is giving out, and there is so much rubble that we cannot rebuild the wall."*
>
> *(v. 10)*

As the people grew more tired, they began noticing how much work was left to be done and how difficult it would be. Funny, nobody had been worried about the rubble when they started. Now it looked insurmountable.

> *Also our enemies said, "Before they know it or see us, we will be right there among them and will kill them and put an end to the work."*
>
> *(v. 11)*

Did you catch that? Suddenly this wasn't just about the work being stopped. Now their lives were on the line.

> *Then the Jews who lived near them came and*
> *told us ten times over, "Wherever you turn, they*
> *will attack us."*
>
> *(v. 12)*

Nehemiah and the others now saw opposition wherever they turned. I suspect the reports were exaggerated, but at this point they were too tired to discern fact from fiction. They were exhausted. They were discouraged.

Well, if I didn't tell you yet, the Book of Nehemiah is not about when the people of God gave up after they built the wall to 20 feet. It's not about how the bad guys got the best of Israel. It's not about the continuing disgrace of the chosen ones, the children of the God of Abraham, Isaac, and Jacob.

It's a story of great, deep, full restoration.

It's a success story.

But you need to know there is a time in every successful renovation when the workers want to go home because the work is so hard.

But God is not done.

Fighting the Lies

How did Nehemiah combat this attack? He adopted some serious measures to protect the people from the opposition's lies.

> *From that day on, half of my men did the work,*
> *while the other half were equipped with spears,*
> *shields, bows and armor.... Those who carried*
> *materials did their work with one hand and*
> *held a weapon in the other.*
>
> *(vv. 16, 17b)*

From that day on, in other words, half the workers' effort was spent guarding. How much do you think that slowed productivity? I'm guessing the work probably slowed by half.

> *Each of the builders wore his sword at his side*
> *as he worked. But the man who sounded the*
> *trumpet stayed with me.*
>
> *(v. 18)*

Say what? Some guy had a trumpet? Uh, OK. Then Nehemiah said to the people,

> *"Wherever you hear the sound of the trumpet,*
> *join us there. Our God will fight for us!"*
>
> *(v. 20)*

So, here's where we stand. Half the people are working; half the people are standing guard. Those who are carrying are only carrying with one hand. Everybody is wearing a sword, and the trumpet guy is with Nehemiah.

If you can keep it straight, you'll see that Nehemiah fought the lies by being diligent and remaining protected.

Being Diligent

When we embark on a renovation project, we too must be diligent—in daily prayer, in the reading of Holy Scripture, and in seeking wise counsel.

We saw that early in Nehemiah's renovation he was diligent in prayer, seeking to understand his people's story in relation to God. Renovation begins in prayers of confession and confusion, which can last for some days. Eventually these become prayers of supplication and desperation, the prayers of "I need this, this, and this, and I need you, God!" Then we move into a disciplined rhythm of prayer: There is still confession and confusion, supplication and desperation, but the prayers now focus more on presence and listening. These prayers allow us to continue encouraging others and making inspired decisions, even when some people are ready to throw in the towel.

We also must remain diligent in reading Scripture. We need to know our story so the things we face don't catch us by surprise. We will be able to respond well, because whatever is happening to us won't seem new at all. Besides helping us respond, Scripture can be a source of power. When Paul wrote to the Ephesians about the spiritual battle we are engaged in, he said that the Word of God is our sword: the sword of the Spirit. I have found in my battles that often I have needed to give the enemy the Word of God. More on this later.

Finally, we must remain diligent in seeking wise, godly counsel. Nehemiah started his renovation project by talking with the king. It stands to reason that he continued to talk with those who would give good, wise counsel. We know he did not work alone, and my guess is that he had some trusted companions who spoke into Nehemiah's life and decisions.

So, we remain prayerful, we study the Scriptures, and instead of withdrawing we engage with other people. This diligence helps us remain strong in the face of opposition.

Protected by the Truth

Besides being diligent, we must protect ourselves, and our best shield is the truth.

When Nehemiah spoke with the king, he requested letters for the governors of every province he would travel through on his way to Jerusalem. These letters granted him safety, but more than that, they gave Nehemiah the authority to procure the materials he needed. All the materials used in rebuilding the wall were the direct result of these letters.

Do you see it? According to the lies of Nehemiah's enemies, he was a dead duck with no hope of finishing his very daunting project. The truth, though, was that Nehemiah had all the permission, provision, and protection needed to see it through to the end. Nehemiah's diligence led to the permission and favors that were needed for the journey. And on that journey, the truth served as his shield.

Remember, God isn't playing games with you. You won't be exposed when you begin your renovation project. You won't be thwarted by the devil's lies or the lies you heard when you were a kid or the ones imposed on you by your parents. You are a child of God!

If you're told that God doesn't want to restore you...if people say you're less than a child of God and a person of worth...if you hear that you won't make it out of addiction or grief or brokenness...well, guess what? Lie. Lie. Lie.

But if you believe that God has hope for you...if you think God can restore you...if you build everything on the foundation of Jesus...Truth. Truth. Truth.

When Nehemiah's people worked on the wall, they knew they would be attacked. But Nehemiah kept the trumpet guy with him. When the attack came, the trumpet blew. Everyone gathered around Nehemiah, and he told them, "Our God will fight for us!" (v. 20).

What was Nehemiah doing there? He was remembering and reminding the people of their story. "Our God will fight for us" was a familiar idea for the people rebuilding the wall, and they all would have recognized it. "Our God will fight for us" was a part of their story. It went back to the time of Moses.

When the people of God had been released from slavery and were headed for the Reed Sea with Pharaoh's chariots and the army hot on their heels, they began to waver a bit. OK, a lot. Moses had been the one with the crazy renovation dream of releasing the people from slavery, so they accused him of bringing them to the wilderness to die. They asked sarcastically,

> *"Was it because there were no graves in Egypt*
> *that you brought us to the desert to die?..."*
> *Moses answered the people, "Do not be afraid.*
> *Stand firm and you will see the deliverance the*
> *LORD will bring you today. The Egyptians you*

see today you will never see again. The LORD
will fight for you; you need only to be still."
(Exodus 14:11, 13-14)

Then, as the people of God watched, the Reed Sea miraculously became a dry road.

Nehemiah and his friends, remembering the story, knew this wasn't the first fight the people of God had faced, and it wouldn't be the last. And ultimately the battle was not theirs; it was the Lord's. Sometimes we, like Nehemiah, have to blow the trumpet and remind each other of the truth found in our story.

A couple weeks into my daughter Phoebe's first-grade year, we received a call from school. It was Phoebe. She wanted to come home.

Did Phoebe need to come home? No. Did she cry some? Yes. Did she go back to class? Yes. Did she keep working hard? Yes. Why did Phoebe's sweet teacher allow her to call home? So Phoebe could hear a little truth.

You are brave. You are strong. You can do this. We are still with you in this. Two more hours and you can come home.

Jenny Youngman, the worship pastor at our church, wrote a song based on Nehemiah and on Phoebe's call home, as a way of giving courage to the people of God. She called it "Brave and Strong."

When the enemy surrounds
and taunts you with his lies,

When you feel like giving up
    and realize that you're tired,
When defeat has robbed your joy
    and you don't know where you stand;
Is the cause worth fighting for anymore?
    Sing it out my soul,

You are brave and you are strong,
You are known and you are loved,
No weapon formed against you
Will stand against our God.

When your courage comes like rain
    on a dry and thirsty heart,
And you find your strength again
    and you remember who you are;
You're a child of the Living God,
    you are more than a conqueror,
You are pressed but never crushed,
    sing out, my soul,

You are brave and you are strong,
You are known and you are loved,
No weapon formed against you
    Will stand against our God....

Our God will fight for us,
Our God will fight for us,
    the enemy will run.

This song has become an anthem for our church, as we try to go where God wants. It has become a trumpet call for us when we are tired and are starting to believe the lies. We sing it loud and with courage, because we know our story. We know that the lies are a part of the story from the beginning, but we know that the truth always wins.

Whenever and however the lie was sown in your life, whether it was as a middle-schooler or a middle-ager, God has a plan for your rescue. The rescue is a renovation, in which all the broken parts are repaired and all the lies of the serpent are crushed underfoot.

God knows your whole story—the apples eaten and the insults believed. God has something else to say to you. You are a child of God and a person of worth. You are brave and you are strong. God will fight for you.

5.

Inviting Others
to Come Home

5. INVITING OTHERS TO COME HOME

My God put it into my heart to assemble the
nobles, the officials and the common people
for registration by families. . . . Ezra praised the
LORD, the great God; and all the people lifted
their hands and responded, "Amen! Amen!"
Then they bowed down and worshiped the LORD
with their faces to the ground.

(Nehemiah 7:5a; 8:6)

I'm not much of a craftsman, but I made something. Once. Rachel and I had been married just a few months, our first Christmas as a married couple was fast approaching, and I really wanted to give her a lasting gift. You know, something that decades later would cause her to say, "Remember that first Christmas when you gave me...?"

I didn't want to just purchase something either. I wanted it to be personal, from my heart and hands. I decided to make her a coffee table. After all, what says love and sentimentality like a sturdy piece of living room furniture? I employed the help of a friend who was a gifted craftsman, and over the course of a couple months we had built a unique, original creation. Looking back, maybe it wasn't the most attractive coffee table of all time, but it was from the heart, my heart. I wrapped it and moved it under the Christmas tree.

When Christmas morning came, the anticipation was almost too much to handle. Well, at least for me. Rachel opened the present and said, "It's a..."

I finished her sentence: "It's a coffee table!"

"Oh," she said. "I wasn't expecting a coffee table."

Exactly! I had succeeded. OK, maybe Rachel wasn't all that excited about it. Maybe it lasted only a short time in our living room before she slyly replaced it with something more to her liking. But what Rachel lacked in excitement, I made up for with mine. And I found myself wanting to share that excitement with others.

When we had visitors, if they didn't quickly notice the coffee table, I would point it out to them. "What do you think about that coffee table?" I would casually ask.

They would say, "It's nice" or some version of that. I would beam with pride, thinking: *I made it. I created it. I dreamed it, and now I was getting to share it.*

Nehemiah's Coffee Table

We have been following the story of Nehemiah, a man called by God to rebuild the broken-down walls of Jerusalem. As we have walked through this rich story, we've been challenged to see the ways in which each of us, as the Bible says, is a spiritual house. Hearing the story, we have realized and admitted that we, too, are in need of renovation. We need something new to happen in us; we want it. But it's not a do-it-yourself project. It's a work that only God can do. And if you've made it this far in the book, there's a chance you are open to whatever beautiful thing God wants to do in you.

As soon as we open ourselves up to God's renovating work, we will begin to hear the naysayers, on the outside and in our own heads. Nehemiah fielded and deflected criticism from others in his renovation project. We heard from his naysayers. The characters Sanballat and Tobiah mocked the whole idea of rebuilding the wall around Jerusalem. They stood next to piles of burnt rubble and said, "Are you really going to bring life back into this mess?" As we learned in the last chapter, Nehemiah chose to remain under the protection of God's truth and to remain diligent and attentive to God's voice.

Because Nehemiah did those things, the project continued until its completion. That's right; the wall was finished! What had begun as a dream in the broken heart of the king's cupbearer was now a reality. If you happened to arrive in Jerusalem after the wall was finished, you might have admired the wall, but there is no way you could know all that had gone into it. But we know.

We met Nehemiah and spent time with him. We were there when he lay on the ground and cried. We were there when he found the courage to ask the king for help. We were there when his courage faltered and he went on nighttime reconnaissance missions, telling no one of his intentions. We were there when things went well and when people wanted to throw in the towel. Now, finally, the last doors in the wall had been finished, and Nehemiah was beaming. Can you imagine how he felt?

Have you ever worked so long and hard on a project—a puzzle, a home improvement project, maybe even a coffee table—that when you completed it, along with your sense of overwhelming joy you also, strangely, felt a sense of loss? Maybe the project took on a personality of its own, and you hated saying goodbye to something you had devoted a season of your life to. Sometimes in this strange melancholy, your heart is moved to share the achievement.

Sharing Your Renovation with Others

When renovation is taking place in your life, there comes a time when you become less focused on the thing being restored (you) and increasingly focused on the impact that your renovation can have on others. This is what happens when God remakes us.

I'm hoping it was clear in my coffee table story that I was joking about my craftsmanship and that people were mostly unimpressed by my creation. What wasn't a joke, though, was my natural sense of wanting to share it. Nehemiah spent quite a long time planning, working, and building. At the conclusion of it all, God put it in the heart of Nehemiah to assemble the people and invite them to share in the achievement. In the same way, at some point you want to share what God has been doing in you.

I was recently at the home of Mark, one of our pastors at Providence Church. Mark has been a friend for years and more recently has partnered in the work that God has called us to at the church. We were at his house for a time of staff worship, planning, and of course eating. Mark has a large, beautiful dining room table, on each side of which are handcrafted wooden benches instead of chairs. The table can easily seat twelve people. Mark, unlike me, was not bragging about it, but his table was getting a lot of attention. You just don't see many tables like that. Being an experienced furniture maker myself, I asked about the story behind the table.

Mark explained that it was built by his dad, Art, who lived in Kansas. Art had recently turned seventy-nine and had been fully retired for about seven years. During that time he had had one major project at the center of his life: building a workshop. For years he had imagined the workshop. As a college professor he had dreamed about the day when he would have his own place to build things. He had sketched it in his mind and on paper. He had carried the plans with him and had shown them to Mark when Mark was in town visiting.

Well, when Art retired he finally built his workshop. It was in a side yard where as a child Mark had spent hours practicing soccer. The workshop was fully equipped and beautiful. I'm sure there must have been folks who wondered about this man in his mid-70s who built a workshop in his yard. A few of them may have thought it was silly to start something new at that stage of life. For those wondering and watching, though, it wouldn't have taken long to see that the project wasn't just for Art; it was about sharing life and new things with the people he loved.

These days the workshop is where grandkids hammer nails into random pieces of scrap wood, creating things for others. It's where Art makes toys for children and gifts for the family. It's where he crafted models of buildings that are being built at an African university. And it's where, in what must have seemed like a wildly ambitious project even to Art, he lovingly constructed the dining room table where I found myself sitting at Mark's that night. Art had made it because Mark's family had outgrown their previous table. You see, the old table would fit Mark's family of six, but it wasn't big enough to welcome guests.

When the church staff gathered at Mark's house for worship and planning that evening, the house was filled with the sounds of praise and conversation. Afterward we ate supper around the table that Art had made. Art was in Kansas, and my guess is that he didn't know about the gathering that night or the people there. But then, the workshop project was never just about Art. It was about his family, of course, which means Mark's family. But that table now welcomes neighbors, friends, and church members. Strangely, mysteriously, beautifully, Art's dream of a workshop in the side yard at a house in Kansas was about you and me.

C. S. Lewis, one of the greatest Christian writers and defenders of the Christian faith, took seriously this scriptural idea that we are God's renovation projects. Inspired by Scottish author and pastor George MacDonald, Lewis wrote,

Imagine yourself as a living house. God comes in to rebuild that house. At first, perhaps, you can understand what He is doing. He is getting the drains right and stopping the leaks in the roof and so on: you knew that those jobs needed doing and so you are not surprised. But presently he starts knocking the house about in a way that hurts abominably and does not seem to make sense. What on earth is He up to? The explanation is that He is building quite a different house from the one that you thought of.... You thought you were going to be made into a decent little cottage: but He is building a palace. He intends to come and live in it Himself.[1]

The coffee table, the workshop, the wall around Jerusalem— these projects are not just about sprucing us up a bit; they're not just about us at all. They are about the living, breathing God doing something through your life that draws others to God. God is making God's dwelling in you, and every time that happens, others will be affected.

When God orchestrates a renovation, it's so God can come live in you and make room for others. If your remodel plan has a little chapel off to one side where God can live and be worshiped, I would invite you to scrap that plan. Remove the chapel. God will live in the whole place, and God will be sharing it with others.

---

1   C. S. Lewis, *Mere Christianity* (New York: Collier Books, 1952), 174.

Homecoming

Nehemiah walked around Jerusalem after the wall had been completed. He hadn't rebuilt the whole city; he had just made further rebuilding seem possible again. Nehemiah wrote, "Now the city was large and spacious, but there were few people in it, and the houses had not yet been rebuilt" (Nehemiah 7:4).

He had seen his renovation completed, and in that moment he noticed how empty it seemed. What was the project about, anyway? It had never been about just building a wall. In fact, if we follow the story in the Book of Nehemiah, we notice that the wall was completed halfway through—in the middle of the book. So the story is not about a wall being rebuilt, but about the return of God's people from exile and captivity.

If we take a step back, isn't that really the theme of the whole Bible? God rescuing God's people? God welcoming us home? It's this ongoing story that culminates in Jesus Christ.

After Nehemiah describes the rebuilding of the wall, he lists all the groups of people who returned. It's a really long list— too long to show here, but you should check it out. It was as if floodgates had opened. Once the wall had been secured, the people of God returned to Jerusalem and to their hometowns. Nehemiah gives us numbers: 49,697 people, plus 246 male and female singers. (Not sure why the singers are listed separately!) Nehemiah names them according to the people from whom they were descended. But whatever the categories, they all were connected to each other and connected to God.

Can you picture it? A group of 49,943—if you count the male and female singers, and I think we should—*plus* almost

8,000 donkeys, horses, mules, and camels. It was a massive homecoming, and it had all been set in motion by the bold vision and faithfulness of Nehemiah.

Can you picture the homecoming that's possible through the rebuilding of your life with God? This is where it gets really exciting and a little risky.

It's exciting because we like to explain the detail of the rebuilding: "Over here, this wall was originally brick. Well, we took that out and added a wood feature." Or, more to the point: "This spot over here, this is where God cleansed me of my addiction—it's where God removed the foundation stones of self and replaced them with Jesus Christ."

And it's exciting when we realize that the project we thought was just about us has in fact spread exponentially to others. We begin to see that God's purposes span way beyond our own horizon. We think about all those who might be affected: our family, our neighbors, even people who may never know our name or recognize the blood, sweat, and tears we put into the project. It's like that table that Art built. People who know nothing about his dreams of a workshop sit down at the table, and they eat, laugh, and are filled.

It's exciting, but it's risky too.

Among those who return, there might be people who once ridiculed us. When Nehemiah threw a party, were Sanballat and Tobiah there? Or there might be people who once spoke lies into our hearts. They might return, too, because God might prepare a place for them. We won't always know their motives. Some might just be curious and want to take a tour of our renovated house. Others might privately be thinking, "That wall will never stand!" They may remember just how messy the rubble of your life once looked.

Those are some of the risks, but the risks are worth taking. Maybe, after all, God's next renovation project involves them.

Coming Back from Exile

To dream about the homecoming, first we have to understand what exile meant. Look at some of the words of those exiled from Jerusalem:

> *By the rivers of Babylon we sat and wept*
> *when we remembered Zion....*
> *If I forget you, Jerusalem,*
> *may my right hand forget its skill.*
> *May my tongue cling to the roof of my mouth*
> *if I do not remember you,*
> *if I do not consider Jerusalem*
> *my highest joy.*
>
> *(Psalm 137:1, 5-6)*

When Nehemiah rebuilt the city, the people had returned to Jerusalem physically, but they weren't all the way home yet. When they arrived in Jerusalem, they asked Ezra the priest to read the law. Their request showed that they hadn't forgotten that the law existed and they existed for God. God wasn't a means to earthly ends. This wasn't just about finding a better place to live; it was about having God live in them. God's renovation project, carried out through Nehemiah, was an avenue for the people to return all the way back to God's heart.

> *Ezra praised the LORD, the great God; and all the people lifted their hands and responded, "Amen! Amen!" Then they bowed down and worshiped the LORD with their faces to the ground.*
> *(Nehemiah 8:6)*

What did the renovation project mean for the people who had been exiled?

They could see, hear, and feel that God had not forgotten them. Sure, they remembered weeping by the rivers of Babylon, but God had not forgotten them. That was clear when they saw what Nehemiah had done. The interesting thing was that they saw the rebuilding but didn't notice Nehemiah himself. Instead, they saw the important thing: that God's memory was good and that God's word was true.

They remembered who they were. In exile, it is easy to forget. When you are far away, you can feel disconnected. When you are broken, you may think you will never feel whole again. Your very identity can begin to change. Thankfully, when the people returned from exile they remembered not just who God was, but who they were: the chosen people of God.

They remembered God's law. Like most of us, the exiled people of God were forgetful, but when they heard Ezra read God's law, they remembered. They shouted, "Amen!" The word of God pierced their hearts, and they remembered. God's law was not just a book of rules to control society; it provided guidance from a God who loved the people enough to rebuild what once had been broken down. God's law was like a manual for those who wanted to be restored, were being restored, and had been restored.

What does a renovation project mean for you?

God remembers you. That's what this renovation is about for you. It's about knowing that God has not forgotten you and will not forget you. God remembers all you have been through, and God remembers you. Your renovation is not just about God fixing your shutters but about God coming to live in you. It's about you coming home.

You must remember who you are. You are not an exile. You are not broken down. You are not destined for weeping. You are a child of God. You are a part of God's family. You are a person of worth. It's in the renovation that we remember who we truly are.

You need to remember God's law. God's law is not about pushing you down and holding you back; it's about setting you free. When we understand that God's law is about our restoration, it causes us to say, "Amen!" and to bow down and worship. The word of God gives us joy. We get to share it with our family around our table. On our really good days, we hear the word of God the way it was heard by the people coming back to Jerusalem, as if for the first time. That's the level of anticipation and receptivity that the people had when Ezra read the law. Let's seek to hear it in the same way.

You get to invite others in! As God renovates your house, get ready to experience the joy of inviting others in. That's the environment that God creates when you give your life to a renovation. Not just at the end of it, but in the midst of it, you invite others. Who will you invite?

*   *   *

After the devastation of Hurricane Katrina in 2005, I traveled with a small disaster relief team to Ocean Springs, Mississippi. I had never seen the kind of wreckage we encountered, where miles and miles of homes were destroyed.

As a part of the relief effort, I worked at the home of Elaina. Elaina was an elderly woman whose home had become so filled with water that she had floated to the top of her living room, then cut a hole in the ceiling and hung on to a rafter until she was rescued. When the waters receded, her home was hardly recognizable. Renovation doesn't even begin to describe what it needed.

The first task facing us was simple. We were to pull out the rubble and pile it up near the street to be taken away. We made another very small pile beside Elaina, who sat in a folding chair in her driveway. This was the pile of things that might be salvaged—a picture, a stuffed animal, a blanket. In the times when I would bring an item to Elaina for her review, I began to learn her story. She was a native Hawaiian. Though only a little girl at the time, she remembered vividly the attack on Pearl Harbor, which left her hometown in grief and devastation. Later, after getting married, Elaina moved to Ocean Springs with her husband, who was in the US armed forces. She now found her life book-ended by two great American tragedies, Pearl Harbor and Hurricane Katrina.

On our last day working at Elaina's home, she called me over and asked for my name and address. She handed me a pad and a pen and asked me to get the names and addresses of the other folks working on her home. I told her that it really wasn't necessary; we were there to serve. Her response surprised me.

"Young man" she said, "I'm not asking so I can send you a thank-you note. It's so I can send you an invitation."

"An invitation?" I asked.

"Yes—to the party I'm going to throw when my home is rebuilt."

I glanced at her house. It was gutted. It had no walls. The brick had been all but washed away. But Elaina saw something I couldn't see. Her life, marked by tragedy, had given her a memory that I didn't have yet. She remembered who she was and what God can do. Elaina had learned that when broken things are restored, when the impossible is made possible, we should do what Nehemiah did: invite others to join us.

It has been over a decade since that trip to Ocean Springs, but when I walk to my mailbox, I still wonder if today will be the day when I get my invitation to Elaina's party. And if you're wondering, I'm going.

6.

The Big Reveal

6. THE BIG REVEAL

They found written in the Law, which the
Lord had commanded through Moses, that
the Israelites were to live in temporary shelters
during the festival of the seventh month.
                                    (Nehemiah 8:14)

The do-it-yourself TV shows give us renovation at warp speed. Before our eyes, a modest home in need of repair and restoration is transformed in an hour, and that's with commercials. Even though the process is sped up, we get to see all the stages of renovation.

We watch with wonder and eagerness as the difficult demolition is undertaken. We are there when the costly unknown factor is found and communicated to the owner. We witness the budget adjustment and the moving forward with a new sense of purpose. We relate to the hard work that is needed. We marvel at the development and execution of the beautiful interior design. We get excited as the finishing touches are added. Each new component builds to the end.

Few would argue that the best part of the show is what happens right before the credits roll. Different shows have different names for of it, but it's always there: the Big Reveal. The curtain is pulled back, and the owner of the home—the one with the original vision and funding—gets to see the finished product. There is often cheering, and more often than not some tears are shed.

The Big Reveal reminds me of baptism. (Only a pastor would say that, right?) The great work has already been done, but we have a communal ritual to acknowledge all that has come before. We mark the restoration that has taken place with a big moment.

I will never forget Julia's baptism. Our church's main focus, what we call our vision, is seeing people who feel disconnected from God and helping them connect with Jesus. Baptism is often the time when we see that vision come to life. Julia had moved from the Pacific Northwest to our area to attend college. She was bright and had a light in her eyes that caused others to connect with her. In our newly formed church that was meeting in a school building, she encountered Jesus, and Jesus changed her life. She was one of the first people baptized at our church. One reason I remember her baptism is because of what happened afterward.

A few weeks after her baptism, Julia met with me in our two-room rented office space. She told me how she had begun to work in the children's ministry at the church. Julia told me she had Matthew, a child on the autism spectrum, in class on several occasions. Previously, Matthew had difficulty finding a church where he would be welcomed. His parents told us they had all but given up on church after all the times when Matthew, following disruptive behavior, had been frowned at, shushed, or sent to the lobby. We were trying our best to provide a supportive environment for Matthew and his family to connect with God and the church. We were a small church, and we were able to devote a lot of attention to Matthew.

What Julia asked me that day changed our new church forever. She said, "What can we do for all the other Matthews in our community?" We were barely able to support Matthew, and here she was, just days after her Big Reveal, dreaming of other children! Her heart was breaking for those she had never even met.

I asked Julia what she thought we should do. She told me, and then she did it. She convened a group of professionals who worked with children with special needs, and one year later we launched Matthew's Ministry. Matthew's Ministry now serves many children with special needs in our community, and it has become one of the most important ministries in our church. And it all happened because Julia, her life still under construction, decided she would invite others to be renovated.

After Nehemiah's Renovation

You never know what your renovation might set in motion! Your renovation leads to the renovation of others. And what happened next with Nehemiah, after his Big Reveal, would change generations of lives.

Remember, Nehemiah's heart had been broken. He cried, he prayed, and finally as an exile in a foreign land he went back home to rebuild Jerusalem. He felt called to reconstruct the mighty wall around the city that had been burned and destroyed. There was opposition, and it was stiff, but his enemies couldn't stand in the face of God's call on Nehemiah and God's plan for God's people.

The wall was rebuilt in fifty-two days. After having their heads down in hard work, the people looked up and saw that the wall was two and half miles around and forty feet high in places. Nehemiah was named governor. The wall was strong again; the people felt strong again. The wall was beautiful again; the people felt beautiful again. Over 49,000 exiles had come home. They looked up, and it was a moment for sure. It was a Big Reveal. It was a marker. It was a baptism.

The people, who had turned their backs on God, who like all of us had messed up, fell on their faces before God. Ezra came and read them their story once again. They gathered around and listened to the words of God. Here's how Scripture describes it.

> *On the second day of the month, the heads of all the families, along with the priests and the Levites, gathered around Ezra the teacher to give attention to the words of the Law. They found written in the Law, which the LORD had commanded through Moses, that the Israelites*

> *were to live in temporary shelters during the*
> *festival of the seventh month.*
> *(Nehemiah 8:13-14)*

Now, this is interesting. This was the Big Reveal, and everyone was back. They were elated and naturally ready for the kind of celebration that comes with such a homecoming. They gathered around, and Ezra reminded them about the festival of booths, a commemorative celebration where everyone moved into a tent or a booth or a lean-to for a season.

So, what's the point? Hang with me.

The Jews had a number of celebrations to help them remember important episodes in their story—high, holy moments, markers on the journey, Big Reveals from years gone by. Just as Christians had Easter and Christmas, Jews had annual remembrances, and one of them was the Festival of Booths. It was a reminder of the time they had been in the wilderness, having escaped from Egypt as slaves, and had lived in temporary housing for years before reaching the Promised Land.

> *The people went out and brought back branches*
> *and built themselves temporary shelters on their*
> *own roofs, in their courtyards, in the courts of*
> *the house of God and in the square by the Water*
> *Gate and the one by the Gate of Ephraim.*
> *(Nehemiah 8:16)*

Huh? is an OK response. Did we hear that right? The city was restored and everything was glistening with the new renovation shine. Thousands of people had come back, connected with family members, and moved back into their homes. It was the Big Reveal. Check out the kitchen, the granite countertops. Ooh, the master bedroom had new paint and lighting, and a beautiful bedspread.

And what did the people do? They built booths, put up tents, and went outside to live? Yes, you heard it right.

> *The whole company that had returned from*
> *exile built temporary shelters and lived in them.*
> *From the days of Joshua son of Nun until that*
> *day, the Israelites had not celebrated it like this.*
> *And their joy was very great.*
>
> *(Nehemiah 8:17)*

They were home, but they decided in the presence of God to remember a time when they didn't have homes. They remembered when they were wandering, when they were fixer-uppers. They celebrated the feast of having no home.

Not only that; the people celebrated like they hadn't in generations, since they had made it to the Promised Land. They ate, drank, and were merry. They partied like it was 1999 B.C.

That's the funny thing about building with God. When we get to the point of celebrating what we have built, God turns our hearts to where we have been . . . and it is there that we remember God's provision and protection.

At the end of a do-it-yourself TV program, they keep showing us what the place was like before. Don't forget how this started. And God does the same thing. At each marker moment, whether it's our baptism or another Big Reveal along the way, God urges us to remember the journey that came before.

Our church finished a new building this year—our first. We had always been a mobile congregation, a wandering church, meeting for eight years in no less than ten locations. The new building is awesome. I am so thankful for it. In fact, I'll bet no one can beat me on thankfulness for our church building. When I come in on Saturdays, I sometimes catch myself saying out loud, "Yep, the chairs are set up," because for eight years I lined up the chairs for worship.

God always turns our hearts to the place we came from. We remember when the air conditioner didn't work in the heat of the summer. We remember that our children's ministry met on school hallway floors. We remember that our sanctuary smelled like a middle school P.E. class. (OK, maybe we can forget that.)

It's good for us to remember our previous buildings, just like it's good for you to remember the place you came from. The act of remembering is not about what we built but about our foundation in Jesus; not about being comfortable but about being faithful; not about bricks and mortar but about people and spirit. Looking back allows us to see the careful protection and precise provision that God has given us along the way.

And so Nehemiah's people put the finishing touches on the walls. They welcomed long-lost relatives back to the city. They had the ribbon cutting and the grand opening. Then they went out and slept in lean-to shelters. They remembered that their ancestors had believed in God's greatness and their beautiful city long before they could see it.

This Is Our Go

Right now you may be in the wandering stage, the wilderness season, the long remodel. Certainly our renovation will not be finished in the sixty-minute length of a TV show. It's helpful to remember that, for the people of God, most of our time is the wilderness season. Even when it seems we have "made it," we remember our time as exiles.

And so, whether we are finished building or still waiting, God calls upon us to celebrate the present goodness.

Imagine all that Nehemiah and the other workers had done to reach the Big Reveal. Think of all the trips to the home improvement store and the boxes that had to be unpacked. And yet, they partied for seven days. They celebrated the present goodness that they were experiencing. They did it in temporary housing to remind themselves that their celebration was not based on accommodations or accoutrements. The celebration was based on the goodness of God—the permission, provision, and protection that God had given and was giving on the journey.

I offer this challenge if you find yourself in the midst of a difficult remodel: Take time to celebrate the present goodness. Celebrate the good that God has given you right now. Look for it. Find it. Claim it.

For years, Rachel and I have used a phrase to remind ourselves of this truth: This is our go.

We share the phrase with each other when we become overwhelmed by what we are going through or consumed by what will happen next. We use it as a way of pulling our beloved one into the present goodness.

This is our go. This is not a dress rehearsal for our life. This is it. This.

It happened just the other day. It was a Saturday. For us, sometimes Saturdays feel like a relay race of getting a kid to this ballgame or that friend's house, running all the errands we neglected during the week, and usually finishing up a work commitment or two. On that particular Saturday, though, the seas were calm. We didn't have anything to do. We loaded up the girls and Zeke the golden retriever and went down to the lake. We made a short hike to the water, and the next thing you know, Zeke and the girls were in the lake. They hadn't planned to swim, but suddenly that's what they were doing. It was unexpected. It was sort of crazy.

Rachel and I sat on a rock with our feet in the water. We held hands. It felt new. I wasn't sure when we had last held hands. We laughed. We celebrated the present goodness.

This is our go. This. All of this. The good, the bad, the crazy, and the calm. That day at the water was a marker, a baptism of sorts.

And because our family is a part of God's family, we don't just soak up the sun and celebrate a beautiful day. It's even better than that. In that moment, we give God thanks and honor. Our hearts feel the warmth of family and fun, but we also get to do what we were made to do: thank God in the simple goodness of right now.

I love that the Israelites, with all they had to do, took a break from those things and celebrated for seven days. They revived a celebration that had been neglected for generations. For a week they did nothing but remember their story and honor God.

What Is to Come

We celebrate what we have built. We remember where we came from. We revel in the present goodness. And then we turn to where we are going. After all, what we have built with our hands, no matter how beautiful, is not permanent.

The first Sunday in our new church building, I was standing in the lobby and the light was shining in. We were between services on what for me was an emotional and chaotic day. A friend approached, someone who had been on the long journey with me. There were people everywhere, the parking lot was packed, and we had just had a powerful worship service.

He said, "So, what's next?"

"Huh?" I said.

"What's next?" he repeated.

I wanted to punch him. It was our first Sunday in the building. What's next? Couldn't we just enjoy what we had done?

Then I realized that God always turns our hearts toward where we are going and what is to come. As Christians, whenever we celebrate buildings we are reminded that no earthly dwelling is permanent.

Jesus knew it. When he told the disciples, it made them mad.

> As Jesus was leaving the temple, one of his
> disciples said to him, "Look, Teacher! What
> massive stones! What magnificent buildings!"
>
> "Do you see all these great buildings?" replied
> Jesus. "Not one stone here will be left on another;
> every one will be thrown down."
>
> (Mark 13:1-2)

Jesus wasn't trying to be rude. He was just saying that even the great Temple in Jerusalem was a temporary shelter. There is more to come beyond what we can see and what we can build with our own hands. He was turning our hearts to where we are going.

The author of Hebrews wrote, "Christ is faithful as the Son over God's house. And we are his house, if indeed we hold firmly to our confidence and the hope in which we glory" (Hebrews 3:6)

We have embraced the image that God has given, that I am God's house, that you are God's house. We have admitted that if we are houses we are fixer-uppers. We have claimed that God does great things with broken-down houses, especially those that have their confidence and hope in Christ.

Believe it or not, the earthly tent you live in now will one day be replaced by a better model. Christians live with an expectation that the houses we have here on earth are just a glimpse of what is to come. I was thirty years old when this reality hit me like a ton of bricks.

I was playing on the floor with my two at-the-time little girls when one of them said, "Daddy, your arm is purple." I looked down, and sure enough my right arm was a shade of blue or purple—whatever the color, not the normal one for my arm. It was swelling and tight. I went to the hospital, where, after spending the night and getting many tests, it was determined that I had a blood clot in my arm. I immediately went on blood thinners and was referred to specialists.

One year later, struggling with discomfort, I was still waiting to hear how they could fix me. That was actually the way I talked about it. I kept waiting for a phone call to tell me the type of surgery or treatment that would get me back to normal. It was a long year. Rachel gave me shots. My activities were limited. I was frustrated.

Then one day I got the call. It was from the head of vascular surgery at our best hospital. He said, "I can't fix it."

"Say that again, Doctor."

"I can't fix it."

I would have to live with the infirmity for the rest of my life. Well, the rest of my life here. I wouldn't get back to normal. Thirty years old and suddenly, physically, I wasn't getting any better. I struggled with the diagnosis. I thought surely there was something I could do.

Some months later I was back with the doctor, sitting on a cold metal examination table. I voiced my thought from months before.

"Surely there's something I can do."

"As a matter of fact," he answered, "I have thought of something you can do."

He explained that the major thoracic vein in my right arm was permanently blocked, and veins are what take blood back to the heart. So, much of my discomfort was the result of not enough blood leaving my arm. The doctor told me that if I simply raised my right hand and arm above my head, gravity would cause blood to flow back down through my smaller veins.

I said, "Let me get this straight. The best thing I can do for my condition is to lift my arm up into the air—the way someone might volunteer to ask a question or maybe even raise their hand to the sky in worship?"

Yes, he assured me. That was exactly what he was saying.

Sometimes the people in my church see me doing this during the worship service. I remind them that I'm simply trying to get the blood out of my arm. Of course, that's not entirely true. When I raise my arm, it reminds me that God alone has the power to restore me. It reminds me that I'm a spiritual house, and my physical house is just temporary. It reminds me of where I've been and gives me confidence and hope in where I'm going.

I wonder if God puts us in a temporary house for the same reason that God's people went to temporary houses after the wall was rebuilt in Jerusalem. Time in a tent reminds us of God's provision and protection. It causes us to be still in this moment. It moves our hearts to give thanks and honor to God. It keeps us looking forward, because there is more to come.

God wants to do some amazing things in your life right now. They will lead to something that you and I have yet to experience. The Big Reveal, a Great Renovation.

I'll see you at the party.

ACKNOWLEDGMENTS

Thank you.

To the people of Providence Church. Wow. I feel like I have grown up with you. Okay, I'm still growing up. You have grown me up. You have supported, encouraged, challenged, and pushed me to live into my calling. Mostly, you have loved me. You have shown me the love of Christ.

To the staff of Providence Church: Dan, Allison, Jenny, Jeana, Sheila, Angela, Pierce, Steffi, Mary Jo, Jennie, Jeff, Jeff. Best team ever. Thanks for helping me be better every day.

Thank you, Susan, Ron, and Abingdon Press friends. Thanks for believing in me and working so hard to get these words out.

To the pastors I live in covenant with: Bryan, Chip, Travis, Ryan, Lee, and Stephen. Thanks for the constant calls and texts. Keep them coming.

To Mark: Thank you for praying over and helping form the words in these pages. Thank you for sharing ministry with me.

Thank you, Gary and Rhonda, for treating me as your son. You have supported me every step.

Thank you, Mom and Dad. You, too, have treated me as your son, because I really am your son. You have taught me about grace all these years. Dad, thanks for showing me what a man of God looks like. Mom, thanks for confirming my call over and over again.

Thank you to my brother, Andy. The adventures behind us and the adventures ahead are in every word I write.

Thank you, Mary. This book is dedicated to you because your awesomeness abounds.

Thank you, Lydia. You give me great joy, and I still consider you my greatest wonder.

Thank you, Phoebe. Every day you make me feel great.

Dad loves you three.

Thank you, Rachel. My story is our story. I love you with everything I got. And I think you are really pretty.

Thank you, Jesus. You saved my life. I want to be a part of sharing your great name with the world.

The Connected Life
Small Groups That Create Community

This handy and helpful guide describes how churches can set up, maintain, and nurture small groups to create a congregation that is welcoming and outward-looking.

Written by founding pastor Jacob Armstrong with Rachel Armstrong, the guide is based on the pioneering small group ministry of Providence United Methodist Church in Mt. Juliet, Tennessee.

978-1-5018-4345-7
978-1-5018-4346-4 eBook

 Abingdon Press™

Available wherever fine books are sold.